THE LIVING WORD

W.H.D. Rouse and the Crisis of Classics in
Edwardian England

by

Christopher Stray

Bristol Classical Press

Cover illustration: W.H.D. Rouse in the garden at Histon Manor, ca. 1932. Rouse used a scythe to cut grass and weeds there, but it also evokes the motto 'Tempora mutantur' which he chose for the Association for the Reform of Latin Teaching (ARLT), which he founded in 1913. The square on the wall behind is a sundial presented to him by the ARLT after his retirement in 1928.

First published in 1992 by
Bristol Classical Press
an imprint of
Gerald Duckworth & Co. Ltd
The Old Piano Factory
48 Hoxton Square, London N1 6PB

© 1992 by Christopher Stray

A catalogue record for this book is available
from the British Library

ISBN 1-85399-262-3

Printed in Great Britain by
Booksprint, Bristol

Contents

Preface

Anyone who has cause to investigate the faded glories of Victorian and Edwardian classical education is likely to encounter a handful of men whose lives and work encourage, even demand, further enquiry. Among these are the first editors of the Loeb Classical Library, T.E. Page of Charterhouse and his friend W.H.D. Rouse, Headmaster of the Perse School, Cambridge. An account of Page has already been given by Niall Rudd in his *T.E. Page: Schoolmaster Extraordinary* (Bristol Classical Press, 1981). The present memoir has two aims: to provide a complementary portrait of Rouse, and to set the careers of both men in the context of contemporary English culture and society. During the decades of their active lives – from the 1870s to the 1920s – radical changes in this larger context impinged irresistibly on the smaller world of classically-educated gentlemen to which both belonged. Page and Rouse, in fact, lived through, and influenced the course of what could be claimed to be the last major crisis of classical studies in England: a crisis in which Classics was detached from its central place in English high culture. In the debates on the classical curriculum which followed the passage of the 1902 Education Act, Rouse played a part which was at once larger and more marginal than that of Page. This marginality, indeed, makes his career a particularly fruitful vantage point from which to assess the progress of those debates. What follows represents an attempt to situate Rouse within this wider context.

Acknowledgements

I would like to thank those who answered my questions or contributed information: Keith Barry, archivist of the Perse School; John Mitchell, Christ's College, Cambridge, the historian of the school; Frank Stubbings, Emmanuel College, Cambridge; John Hazel and Wilf O'Neill of the Association for the Reform of Latin Teaching; Rouse's pupils Cyril Peckett and Arthur Eagling; Frank Lockwood's pupil Arthur Munday; Mrs Molly Lockwood and her son (Rouse's godson) Dr Michael Lockwood; Mr J. Skirrow, librarian of the Baptist Missionary Society; the Revd B.R.White, Regent's Park College, Oxford; and Miss Jennifer Goodwin, archivist, Linguaphone Institute. Professor Niall Rudd read through drafts of the text and made a number of valuable suggestions. Subventions in aid of publication were originally provided by the following, to whom I should like to express my thanks: the Association for the Reform of Latin Teaching, the Loeb Classical Foundation, and the Perse School. When this subsidy was lost owing to the take-over of the Bristol Classical Press in 1991, the book was rescued by further subventions from Clive Rouse and from the Master and Fellows of Christ's College, Cambridge. Without these, this memoir would not have seen the light: I thank them also. My greatest debt is to Mr and Mrs Clive Rouse, whose benevolent hospitality made it possible for me to work on Rouse's papers under ideal conditions.

Acknowledgements

Introduction

The format of the Loeb Classical Library – text and translation on facing pages, with a minimum of annotation – is now something widely taken for granted. In 1911, when T.E. Page and W.H.D. Rouse began their editorial work, it was not. Yet in retrospect, it is clear that the conception reflected in this format was very much of its time. One of the results of the late nineteenth-century shift from the use of the Classics as a mirror of current opinions to their analysis in their own terms was the increasing use of plain texts. The role of the editor was central, but unobtrusive.[1] Here the German firm of Teubner had early established a lead; Charles Cannan of Oxford University Press (OUP), whose achievement was to combine the resources of Oxford scholarship with the distribution facilities available in London, followed with the Oxford Classical Texts, which began to appear in 1898. At about the same time, the Home University Library, which OUP took over in 1906, expanded successfully into a new market, catering for the adult learner. The Loebs bridged the gap between these spheres, offering an accurate plain text for scholarly use on the left-hand page, a readable and accurate translation on the right. In thus acknowledging the existence of a readership interested in, but not wholly competent to read, classical literature, the Loebs reflected contemporary changes in education and society.[2] They form part of a transitional era in the history of Classics, between an age in which elite education could almost be equated with classical learning, and the present age, in which the subject has been marginalised to such an extent that recent government proposals for a national curriculum do not even mention it.

The late Victorian and Edwardian eras are too easily seen as possessing a comfortable and massive stability. The serried ranks of scholarly volumes produced at the time help to maintain the illusion. R.C. Jebb's *Sophocles* (1883-96) brought him a knighthood; *A History of Classical Scholarship* (1908) earned the same honour for J.E. Sandys. The massive volumes of *The Cambridge Bibliography of English Literature* contain the latter's chapters on scholars, reflecting and confirming the centrality of classical

1

scholarship in an embedded tradition which combined learning and liberal education. Yet despite their solidity, these heavy tomes represented the twilight flight of the owl of Minerva. Their learning was already under challenge from newer kinds of scholarship. Comparative philology had become largely independent of its roots in classical study and was turning into the new science of linguistics. Anthropology was being brought to bear on Greek drama and religion at the hands of the 'Cambridge Ritualists': the group of scholars, centred on Jane Harrison and including F.M. Cornford, A.B. Cook and Gilbert Murray, whose work on the ritual origins of Greek tragedy, as on other aspects of Greek life, revealed a darker and less comforting world than the Olympian serenity still dominant in English preconceptions about classical Greece.[3] At the same time the relationship between scholarship and gentlemanly amateurism was progressively weakened, as men like Henry Nettleship and Ingram Bywater at Oxford, and H.A.J. Munro and A.E. Housman at Cambridge, fostered a narrower and more rigorous study of classical language and literature.[4]

The world of the classically-educated gentleman persisted, of course. The Oxford and Cambridge colleges, together with the public schools, the London clubs and the semi-rural enclave of St James', constituted an exclusive male world where Latin and Greek verses were composed in leather armchairs. Both Page and Rouse fitted comfortably into this world, as did many other scholarly schoolmasters in a period when the divide between school and university teaching was much less marked than it is now. Yet the world of club and college to which they belonged, though coherent, was neither homogeneous nor unchanging. Clubland itself offered a home for a variety of opinions. Page spent his last night at the Reform Club, favourite meeting-place of the Liberals, chuckling at the stories of the novelist Frank Swinnerton;[5] at the Athenaeum, Rouse on occasion talked to Dean Inge of St Paul's, whose Toryism was even more extreme than his own.

The changing emphasis in classical study – from liberal education to learning – can be seen by looking at the work Page and Rouse produced. When the first Loebs appeared in the autumn of 1912, Page was 62, and had recently retired after 37 years as a housemaster at Charterhouse. Rouse, 13 years his junior, had been Headmaster of the Perse School, Cambridge, since 1902, and had built a boarding house for himself on the outskirts of the town in 1910. Page had published editions of Horace and Virgil in the Macmillan school series, and a commentary on the *Acts of the Apostles*. Rouse's output was at once larger and more varied: a translation of four volumes of Karl Brugmann's Indo-European Grammar, with R.S. Conway; a large book on *Greek Votive Offerings*; manuals of Greek and

Introduction

Latin verse composition; and a history of Rugby School. He had also edited a series of Latin texts for Blackie and *The Year's Work in Classical Studies* for the Classical Association (CA), and was currently Cambridge editor of the *Classical Review*. The disparity in the amount they produced can be explained, in part, by the fact that while Page had a family to support and a boarding house to run, in addition to acting as a town councillor, Justice of the Peace and part-time businessman,[6] Rouse was a bachelor, and until 1910 had not had the responsibility of a house. More significant, however, is the difference in the nature of their output, for it encapsulates more general changes in the content and style of English classical scholarship.

Page and Rouse had both read for the Classical Tripos at Cambridge. But between Page's departure in 1873 and Rouse's arrival in 1882, the Tripos had been reorganised. For some time, accretions of historical and philosophical subject-matter had been added to the core of linguistic and literary study. Now the course was split into two parts: Part I retained the traditional concentration on literature; Part II added to it an array of optional courses on philosophy, history, archaeology and philology. Page fulminated from Charterhouse against the proposals, which he claimed ignored 'the requirements of...the men, who without any desire to pursue any special branch of classical learning, are widely read in classical literature...the sort of men who in the old Classical Tripos would have occupied the first ten places in the first class.' 'The new scheme would', he concluded, give 'a fatal blow...to the study of classics as a liberal ...means of education'.[7] It was this reorganised Tripos which Rouse sat, gaining a First in Part 1, and a better one in Part II, where he was examined in literature and in comparative philology. The breadth of his interests is visible in his correspondence in the 1890s, when he was a fellow of Christ's College. In this correspondence he discusses archaeology and religion with J.G. Frazer and William Ridgeway, and Pali scriptures with E.B. Cowell, the Professor of Sanskrit.

Two somewhat different styles of scholarship then, but with a large overlap in a shared commitment to classical literature as a source of value, an enduring touchstone for aesthetic and moral judgement of the present. And as we shall see, the specialised knowledge in areas like philology and folklore which Rouse acquired were placed at the service of this commitment. Both Page, the son of a provincial bank manager, and Rouse, the son of a Baptist missionary, belonged by education, rather than by birth, to the world of classically-educated gentlemen in which this commitment played a central part. In the Edwardian era, this was a world under attack: for it lay at the heart of an established order which was in crisis. By the 1900s, internal and external pressures for social and educational change, resisted and deflected for a generation since the liberal interlude of the 1860s and 1870s, had become irresistible. In the lengthy public debates which followed the passage of the 1902 Education Act, the public-school classical curriculum became a major target for progressive and radical critics.

How did this crisis come about? To answer that question, we have to go back to the first half of the nineteenth century. In his essay *Christ's Hospital thirty-five years ago*, Charles Lamb recalled with affection the Rev. Matthew Field, who taught him there in the 1780s – one of 'that class of modest divines who affect to mix in equal proportions the gentleman, the scholar, and the Christian'. The career of Classics in nineteenth-century England can be traced in terms of the dissolution of this alliance of learning, religion and social status. The alliance was reinvigorated but, in the long term, weakened, by the influx of German *Wissenschaft* after the lifting of the continental blockade in 1816. Within the Anglican Church, the German romantic conception of philology as the science of linguistic and cultural manifestations of human reason was generally welcomed. The empiricist philosophies of the eighteenth century were seen – wrongly – as having promoted a conception of language as the embodiment of those sensations through which human beings passively received information from the external world; the philology of Franz Bopp and Jacob Grimm, on the other hand, viewed language as an organic entity independent of sense-data and integrated by grammar, its 'inner form'. The science of words, thus conceived, might prove a valuable ancilla to the Word of God; by focusing on the organic form of language, it combated the atomising tendencies of materialism, while by domesticating Reason within its manifestation in language, it offered a powerful defence against rationalism.[8]

The philology which was hailed as a bulwark of established religion, however, eventually became a corrosive force. The criticism which B.G. Niebuhr applied to Roman myths led to the criticism which Friedrich Schleiermacher and D.F. Strauss applied to the Bible.[9] Thus, while classical scholars of conventional theological views might be promoted to bishoprics – as with Charles Blomfield's translation from Cambridge to the see of Chester in 1825 – their less orthodox brethren faced exclusion of a different kind. Charles Badham, the friend of F.D. Maurice and pupil of J.H. Pestalozzi, spent 20 years as a Headmaster before becoming a Professor of Classics in Sydney; F.A. Paley, having converted to Catholicism, made a living first as a tutor to rich Catholic families, later by writing school editions of classical authors and, ironically, by examining for University College London – the 'godless college in Gower Street'.[10] Most notoriously, Connop Thirlwall's attack on compulsory chapel at Trinity College, Cambridge led to his expulsion from that institution. His subsequent preferment to the see of St David's took place only after careful vetting of his theological writings by the Archbishop of Canterbury; his claim to the Primacy itself, it was rumoured, was ruined by his translation of Schleiermacher. Thirlwall's fellow Liberal Anglican, Julius Hare, left Trinity for a rich living in Hurstmonceux, where he spent the rest of his life in devotion to his parishioners and to his enormous library. The long list of his publications after his departure from Cambridge contains not a single item on classical subjects.[11] The journal Hare and Thirlwall had founded (the *Philological Museum*, 1832-3) collapsed when they left Cambridge; an attempt at revival in the 1840s (the *Classical Museum*, 1844-50, edited by a pupil of Niebuhr), folded after several years of financial insecurity. In the continuing absence of an academic career structure, the scholarly community which might have supported such enterprises hardly existed. In the 1850s, the comforting antiquarianism of Dean Trench and the elegancies of Max Müller still held sway in the studies and drawing-rooms of the nation.[12]

As this may suggest, even were intellect to escape the constraining bonds of faith, it was still held captive by the shackles of social convention. The dominant form of classical scholarship which emerged in the public schools and the ancient universities from the 1820s to the 1860s was based on the memorisation of passages from a narrow canon of authors, and their use as a resource for composition. It is customary to contrast this English style of scholarship with its German counterpart, the *Altertumswissenschaft* of F.A. Wolf and C.G. Heyne. Yet they sprang from a common romantic impulse: the concern to understand the thoughts and feelings of the Greeks and Romans through immersion in their literature. On the other hand, England was isolated from the Continent between the 1790s and the 1810s; and the primary sources of the English gentlemanly version of this romantic scholarship are to be found in contemporary English society. The retreat from the public world of mid-eighteenth-century England into the segregated privacy and class consciousness of the the Victorian era was accompanied by a conservative reaction to the Enlightenment and to the French Revolution. The emergence of prosperous moneyed groups alongside the landowning gentry and aristocracy created a confused situation in which novel forms of social and cultural validation were formulated. Verse composition in Latin and Greek combined the romantic focus on the incomparable validity of individual creation with the fussy concern for metrical detail characteristic of the conservatism of the 1790s. This conservative romanticism, it can be argued, lay at the heart of a form of social attainment which marked the solidarity of those in certain social groups, and the exclusion of those without.[13]

In the second half of the century, having lost the original impetus gained from the romantic movement, this tradition was often trivialised into a set of technical puzzles; the challenge to turn an advertisement or a gas bill into elegiacs became its own justification. For most of the thousands of schoolboys who toiled through the public-school classical course, on the other hand, its intricacies remained incomprehensible; metrical discipline led to poetic creation only for a few. Yet for those who attained to excellence in it – men like Benjamin Kennedy, C.S. Calverley, Jebb or T.S. Evans – it helped to maintain a commitment to a vision of moral value. How strong and pervasive this commitment could be is evident in the declaration of Montagu Butler, successively Headmaster of Harrow and Master of Trinity College, Cambridge, who wrote in 1914:

> At Harrow, in Trinity, in Egypt, in the Desert of Sinai, in Palestine, in Greece, in Italy, in France, in Switzerland, in Scotland, on railway journeys, in mountain walks, in solitary hours, in times of sorrow and depression, in times of overflowing happiness, the old habit of making verses, begun almost before Harrow days,…has clung to me as a faithful companion, helping me, however imperfectly, to keep in touch with the thoughts of the wise, the pious, and the pure, and giving a kind of quiet unity to a life of some labours and many distractions.[14]

In the 1870s and 1880s, the Test Acts, which had barred teaching posts at the ancient universities to Nonconformists, were repealed, and celibacy restrictions for college fellowships were removed. Among the results was the accelerated growth of a professional scholarly community at Oxford and Cambridge. As the rate of graduate ordination declined, the comfortable belief of the learned clergyman in permanent truths which were necessarily harmonious aspects of a greater Truth gave way to the don's moralised quest for a truth which was not permanent but progressive, and thus open to discussion and revision.[15] For some men, caught between a faith to which they could no longer subscribe and a scientific naturalism which seemed empty of moral value, the pursuit of truth in the humanities offered a substitute. Here the universities and the public schools were at odds. In the latter, although lay assistants had been relatively common since the late 1850s, the clerical headmaster remained *de rigueur* until the 1900s. The careers of both Page and Rouse have to be viewed against this background. Page, a devout Christian who prayed twice a day, was well aware that other men cynically took orders just before applying for headmasterships; he himself refused several offers of headships in order not to be forced to do the same. Rouse had intended to follow his father into the missionary field, but found himself unable to subscribe to the articles of faith laid down by the Baptist Missionary Society. His inability to enter Anglican orders undoubtedly contributed to his failure to obtain a headship in the 1890s. Page practised his faith and his Classics alongside one another; Rouse ended up turning his commitment to Classics into a secular mission. In the following pages, I hope to identify the sources of this mission, the energies and concerns which sustained it, and its relationship to the crisis of classical studies in late Victorian and Edwardian England.

Early life: Calcutta, Haverfordwest and London (1863-81)

William Henry Denham Rouse was born on the 30th May 1863 in a Baptist mission house in Calcutta. His father George Henry Rouse was at the time Indian Secretary of the Baptist Missionary Society. The child was named after his maternal grandfather William Henry Denham, himself a Baptist missionary and President of Serampore College. The college had been founded in 1818 by the first Baptist missionaries in India, William Carey, Joshua Marshman and William Ward, and had formed the centre of their activities since then.[16] The translation of the Bible into several dozen Indian dialects was an ongoing process which included revision and updating, as well as the printing of Bengali and other grammars. It is significant, in view of young William's later career, that the Baptists laid a heavy emphasis on linguistic and literary scholarship. Denham, a convert from Catholicism to Baptism, had originally made a living as a language teacher, and he made use of his linguistic prowess after he became a missionary. William's paternal grandfather had moved from the country to London in the 1840s so that his son could attend the school at King's College, London;[17] we can assume that George Henry had a reasonable grounding in Latin and Greek.

The early Baptist missionaries were not welcomed by the East India Company and its successors, and were forced initially to establish themselves in the Danish colony in India. They were, for the most part, of lower middle-class origin, and some were claimed to have been associated with political radicalism during the anti-Jacobin alarms of the 1790s. A particular concern was that young clerks sent out to India might become converted to radical beliefs. The suspicion the Baptists aroused in official quarters was not dampened by their approach to missionary work. Their views on the culture of the heathen were firmly on the liberal side in a continuing debate among missionary groups. That is, they believed in taking Indian religious beliefs and scriptures seriously, in order to understand how to convert the population to Christianity. At the beginning of the nineteenth century, their views found some support in Lord Wellesley's policies. His 'College of Fort William', intended to rival Oxford and Cambridge in size and endowment, was founded in Calcutta in 1800 to promote the teaching of Indian languages and civilisation, as well as the usual forms of Western learning. That support, however, was removed by the change of policy signalled by Thomas Macaulay's notorious Minute of 1834, which declared that a shelf of European books was worth the whole of Eastern learning.[18]

In the second half of the century, the spread of newspaper publication in Bengal, some in English, began to affect the style of Bengali literature, which had been relatively stiff and formal. Reporting to the Baptist Missionary Society in the 1890s on his revision of the Bengali Bible (1893-7), the Rev. Rouse declared, 'Now at last we can be direct, immediate and idiomatic at the same time'.[19] It is difficult to resist the conclusion that this vernacular stress in literary evangelism had a powerful influence on his son's doctrine of Direct Method teaching.

George Henry's first period of duty in India was brought to a premature end by illness after only two years. After his enforced return to England, he was appointed Classical and Mathematical Tutor at the Baptist College in Haverfordwest, Pembrokeshire. Here William attended the local grammar school, of which he retained only a few, and not particularly happy memories. To this period can be dated his earliest published work, 'The Haverfordwest SUN' [sic], a handwritten newspaper of which only one issue survives, written on both sides of a sheet of lined paper. The news content is confined to a report remarkable for its conciseness: 'The Rev Dr Davies preached a very nice sermon of [sic] Sunday December 31st, and read the Queen's letter. All listened with both their ears.' The issue also contains the concluding chapters of 'The Boy, who killed three giants', whose hero, somewhat transparently, is named Bill; and a riddle section. This is a tantalising item, as it contains two riddles to which answers are promised 'in our next', and the answers to riddles given in a previous issue. The answer to Riddle III, for example, is 'A woman going over a bridge with a bucket of water upon her head'.[20]

In 1872, the Rouses returned to Calcutta, where the Rev. Rouse had been appointed pastor of the Circular Road Baptist church. William was now sent to 'The Doveton College Academic and Parental Institution', where he received a rather haphazard education. In a published reminiscence which appeared in 1898, he recalled being in a class with two other English boys, Armenians, Parsees and a variety of other races. The curriculum included short sections of the Latin grammar, learnt by heart, and couplets of Ovid, dictated with translation; William was taught the elements of Greek at home by his father.[21]

In 1880 the family came back to London on leave. William was sent to Regent's Park College, a Baptist training college which his father had attended in its original home in Stepney in the late 1850s. The college records reveal that William was top of his class in New Testament Knowledge, with a mark of 81%. More significantly, they make it clear that he attended the college as a lay student: in other words, he was preparing for university rather than for mission work.[22] In 1881, he gained a scholarship to Christ's College, with which he was to be closely associated until his death in 1950.

Undergraduate, don and schoolmaster: Cambridge, Bedford, Cheltenham and Rugby (1882-1901)

Rouse's progress through the Tripos has already been mentioned. In Part II, he was examined in literature and in comparative philology, and was given firsts in both. His mentor in philology was the Master of Christ's College, John Peile, who had been largely responsible for encouraging the teaching of Sanskrit at Cambridge. Together with Conway and Peter Giles,[23] Rouse became one of his star pupils, and in 1888 was elected to a six-year fellowship at Christ's College. His scholarly work in the next few years reflected exactly the new directions in classical study encouraged by the reorganised Tripos. He and Conway took over from Joseph Wright the task of translating Brugmann's monumental Indo-European Grammar. Wright's translation of Volume I appeared in 1888, and Conway and Rouse's translation of the following four volumes between 1891 and 1895. He also embarked on the collation of manuscripts of Nonnos' *Dionysiaca*: a Greek epic in 48 books, written in Egypt at the end of the third century AD, devoted to the exploits of Dionysus. This appears to have been done at the behest of the orientalist W. Robertson Smith, and the latter's death in 1894 led to the cancellation of the project, but Rouse returned to Nonnos in his retirement.[24] At the same time, he worked on a large-scale study of Greek votive offerings, which eventually gained him a LittD and was published by the University Press in 1902. In the late 1880s and early 1890s, this brought him into contact with several scholars who were working in related areas: Cook, Frazer and Ridgeway. Ridgeway became a close friend, and several letters testify both to their constant exchange of information and ideas, and also to their shared views on university politics. Both were passionately opposed to the admission of women to Cambridge and to the abolition of 'Compulsory Greek', and both became violently anti-German in the 1910s. Ridgeway's best-known book is his *Early Age of Greece*

11

(1901), but he also published on the origins of the horse and on ancient currency. His work shows the influence of the Cambridge Ritualists, though he was not a member of the group (his relentless opposition to academic women would surely have made relations difficult, to say the least, with Jane Harrison, the group's leading light). Ridgeway's letters to Rouse make it clear that the traditional concern for the detailed linguistic analysis of texts, rather than for their relation to myth, religion and society, was still dominant in Cambridge Classics. In the 1890s, he still felt out of place there, accepted neither by the archaeologists nor by the linguistic scholars. His difficulties were in part a matter of personality. Ridgeway was both an inveterate intriguer and a fierce polemicist who loved a fight, and once seized of a theory, was unwilling to be deterred by inconvenient facts or critical comment.

In 1894 Rouse's fellowship lapsed. Peile wrote to him to congratulate him on 'breaking the necks of two such giants' (i.e., the translation of Brugmann and the work on votive offerings), and declared that 'no-one who has had so brief a tenure has...made a better use of it'.[26] But there were no college teaching posts available, and an academic career was ruled out. Rouse's predicament was a general one. So few college fellows vacated their fellowships for church livings, as had happened a generation before, that those who won the new six-year fellowships were often unable to carry on at the end of their tenure. J.W. Headlam, who sat Part II of the Tripos in the same year as Rouse, had the same experience when his fellowship at King's College lapsed in 1896. Headlam worked as one of Her Majesty's Inspectors of Education (HMI), and then as Staff Inspector in the new Board of Education; on the outbreak of war in 1914 he became Assistant Director of the Political Intelligence Unit at the War Office. When he applied, unsuccessfully, for the new chair of Ancient History at Cambridge in 1899, he had already been away from Cambridge for too long to stand much chance of election.

By this time Rouse had had several years' experience of schoolmastering. After two not very happy years at Bedford, in 1890 he had moved to Cheltenham College, which he found more congenial. The staff included several modern language teachers who were enthusiasts for the use of the Direct Method in modern language teaching: that is, teaching a language by speaking it. The impetus for this movement had come from Germany, and in particular from the campaigning enthusiasm of Wilhelm Viëtor, whose polemical pamphlet *Language teaching must start afresh! (Der Sprachunterricht muss umkehren!)* appeared in 1882 under the pseudonym 'Quousque Tandem'. Viëtor's pamphlet was subtitled *A contribution to the question of stress and overwork in schools*, and formed part of a contemporary German debate on that subject. But since one of his major targets was the stultifying study of grammar, the contemporary teaching of Latin and Greek inevitably took much of the weight of his attack.[27] For like-minded English schoolmasters, the views of Viëtor and his followers offered an escape from the inferiority complex which led many teachers of French and German to seek respectability by treating them as dead languages. A few months before Rouse arrived in Cheltenham, the school had been the venue for a conference of the reformers, so that he will probably have been made aware of the issues. While at Cheltenham, he was engaged by Dorothea Beale, Headmistress of Cheltenham Ladies' College, to teach Greek to a sixth-form class, and was clearly a great success. On hearing the news of his impending move to Rugby in 1895, she wrote, 'I live in fear of a general exodus to Rugby'; and in the following year, 'your class have fallen to pieces, and I can't get them to take anyone else'.[28]

Fig. 1 Crumbs from the Headmaster's plate. Cartoon dating from Rouse's days as a master at Rugby (1895-1902). The tall figure is the Headmaster H.A. James; Rouse is second from left, begging for crumbs in canine fashion. The cartoonist is D.C. Bolton (1884-1928), a pupil at the school from 1897 to 1902. [Perse School Archives]

13

In 1895, Rouse's Headmaster H.A. James was appointed Headmaster of Rugby, and took Rouse with him. In a testimonial he gave when Rouse was himself applying for headships, James wrote that he had been secured for Rugby because he was 'a quite exceptionally good teacher, especially for the ablest of his pupils'.[29] When he moved to Rugby, Rouse was in his early thirties, with several years' experience of classical teaching and a scholarly record which was fairly brief but already impressive. Though not a housemaster in the ordinary sense, he became 'Tutor to the Town', in charge of facilities for dayboys.[30] Among his pupils was the young Arthur Ransome, whose father had moved to Rugby so that Arthur could attend the school. Rouse discovered that Arthur had poor eyesight, and had his eyes tested; he encouraged him to write; and offered to coach him for entrance to Oxford. The reading of J.W. Mackail's biography of William Morris, to which Ransome attributed his conversion to a life of writing, may well have have been the result of a suggestion from his form-master.[31] Rouse himself was busy writing, and the results had already begun to appear before he left Rugby for the Perse in 1902. In 1898 his history of the school appeared, which remains the standard treatment for the period up to Thomas Arnold's death. It was based on considerable research in the school archives, and led him to the conclusion that the important changes in direction at Rugby had been made not by Arnold, but by his predecessor Thomas James. In the following year, he published collections of classical portraits for use in teaching: photographs of statues and busts of statesmen, poets and others, each accompanied by brief notes. These publications might be taken as evidence not just of his concern with the material contexts of ancient literature, but also of his anthropological interests. Earlier in the 1890s, he had corresponded with Francis Galton about the recording of facial patterns. Two books of his which appeared in 1899 were both more traditional and yet more radical. In that year the Clarendon Press published his *Demonstrations in Latin Elegiac Verse*, while a parallel volume on Greek Iambics appeared from the Cambridge Press.

When the Latin volume was submitted to the Oxford Press, it had impressed Charles Cannan, Secretary to the Delegates, who described it as 'a good book…its plan as far as we know entirely novel'.[32] In both books, Rouse began by dissecting the process of verse composition into its component parts, then took a series of English texts and showed in detail how one might go about composing Latin or Greek versions. They were based, as he tells us in the Preface to the volume on Greek Iambics, on his 'composition lectures of the previous ten or twelve years'. An indication of the technique Rouse had developed in these lectures can perhaps be gained from what he tells us about the organisation of the book: 'as far as possible all information is evolved from the class by questions, *more Socratico*'. Rouse himself was conscious of the novelty of his method, but confident of the results: 'I am not aware that this method of teaching has been advocated before, and I never knew anyone who used it. If they try it, they may be sure that they will find their work more interesting and their pupils more interested...the real advantage is, that we not only show the result to a class, but the way in which it is attained.'[33] Here are several of the central features of the methods which Rouse made the foundation of his teaching at the Perse in the 1900s: conversation, question and answer, the Socratic method; eliciting knowledge from pupils rather than simply injecting it into passive subjects; and approaching classical literature from the inside by creating in Latin and Greek. In short, these two books represent an attempt at a radical renewal of a nineteenth-century English tradition which had become at best tiresome, at worst oppressive, for the majority of pupils.

This does not exhaust the list of Rouse's activities in the 1890s. He was also an energetic and outspoken member of the Assistant Masters' Association (AMA), founded in 1891 to defend the interests of public-school assistants against heads and governing bodies. At that time, assistant masters had almost no security of tenure, and it was not unknown for an incoming headmaster to sack some or even all his staff and replace them with his own connexions. Public opinion, however, was slowly moving against the more brutal aspects of this relationship, and a series of blatant and heavily-publicised cases helped the AMA to secure some amelioration of the assistants' lot. Rouse was Secretary for several years, resigning when he became Headmaster of the Perse in 1902, and conducted a vigorous publicity campaign among Members of Parliament. It was probably through the AMA that he first met Page, also a committed defender of the rights of assistants. Page seems to have been recruited by Rouse, and soon became Chairman of the Association.

Such activities, of course, carried their penalties for the outspoken assistant who wanted to become a headmaster. Both men are likely to have suffered from their public involvement with the AMA in the 1890s, but they also faced the problem of ordination: the persisting convention that the headmaster of a public school should be a clergyman. Both were Christians, though in Rouse's case, at least, it is not easy to say of what kind. Page, as has already been mentioned, was a devout believer: why did he not take Anglican orders? The most likely explanation for this is that his youth and early manhood coincided with the bitter debates which followed the publication in 1862 of *Essays and Reviews*. This collection of modernist theological essays brought charges of blasphemy upon several of its contributors. One of them, Frederick Temple, was at the time Headmaster

15

of Rugby; when his appointment as Bishop of Exeter was announced in 1869, several other bishops attempted to block his consecration because of their opposition to his theological opinions. The violent controversy stirred up by *Essays and Reviews* deterred many young men from taking the plunge into ordination. One such was the Liberal MP Theodore Walrond, Temple's favoured candidate to succeed him as Headmaster of Rugby in 1869. Walrond told Archibald Tait – Archbishop of Canterbury, and himself a former Headmaster of Rugby – that he had hesitated over ordination at a time when 'many good men appeared to be uneasy...under burdens such as subscription' (i.e., the declaration that the candidate accepted the 39 Articles of the Anglican Church). Tait agreed to confer orders on Walrond just before he applied for the Rugby headmastership.[34] Whatever the merits of this particular case, many men adopted the same course in complete cynicism, and thus brought down on themselves the righteous anger of men like Page, who saw their own ambitions frustrated because they were laymen. On hearing of Rouse's appointment to the Perse, Page wrote to him 'I saw with mixed feelings that you had got the Perse School...you may do a world of good by driving into the minds of intelligent men the scandal and ruin caused by the present ecclesiastical government of schools. Men like Jebb and the Master of Trinity and many Cambridge dons on governing bodies might do a deal but they have not a particle of pluck or honesty among a dozen.'[35] Page had been asked more than once to apply for headships, but on each occasion the necessity of ordination had presented an insuperable obstacle. Most galling, perhaps, was his failure in 1897 at Charterhouse, the school which he had served loyally for almost a quarter of a century. He predicted the failure in a letter to Rouse: 'The Governing Body meets on Thursday and my name will undoubtedly be brought before them but whether they will have the courage to be just is another question...'.[36] Meanwhile Page was forced to watch other men rising with apparent ease: 'You'd better not place too much trust in the Headmaster of Harrow, he owes his own rapid promotion entirely to taking orders and speaking about church questions.'[37] Looking back in 1910, Page wrote to Rouse, 'This year, when I retire at Christmas, will see the end of my career. It would be folly not to allow, that I feel bitter at the insulting treatment I have received whenever I have applied for any post; and above all, from my own governing body, which desiring mediocrity, has probably got it.'[38]

It is difficult to know how much his lay status contributed to Rouse's failure to obtain a headship. But fail he certainly did in the late 1890s, despite several attempts, and although he had the support of some influential backers. Among those providing testimonials were one of the most respected headmasters of the day, Edwin Abbott of the City of London School; Edward Cowell and Peile, the two leading Cambridge Sanskritists; Ernest Gardner, Professor of Classical Archaeology at Oxford; the philologist W.W. Skeat; Ridgeway; and J.S. Reid, who became Professor of Ancient History at Cambridge in 1899. Rouse's applications declared that 'I cordially agree with that system of education which places moral and religious training first; intellectual training second; and which uses the games as a means strictly subordinate, yet invaluable, for the development of courage, endurance and public spirit.' He added that while not in orders, he was not indifferent to the religious side of a schoolmaster's work: 'My reasons for not taking orders are technical, not religious.' Despite this array of supporters and carefully-worded applications, however, he failed of success at the King's Grammar School, Warwick, in 1896, at Tonbridge in 1898, and at Aldenham in 1899. At King Edward VI, Birmingham, he was one of the final two candidates considered. His last application was to St Paul's, made in 1905 after two difficult years at the Perse; here again he failed at the last fence, having reached the shortlist of three candidates.[39] When he did succeed, it was at a small and run-down grammar school with close ties to his own university. The rest of his teaching career was spent at the Perse School, Cambridge, which became the site of his 'great experiment': the revitalisation of the nation through the reform of classical teaching.

The precarious experiment: Rouse at the Perse (1902-6)

In 1902 the Perse Grammar School's future was, to put it mildly, unsettled. In the previous year, the County Council had opened a new secondary school which undercut the Perse's fees by at least 50%. The new school was also better equipped to teach commercial subjects, and the commercial side of the Perse was closed in 1901. One of Rouse's advisers, Herbert Millington of Bromsgrove School, urged to him to think twice before accepting an offer:

> Look warily before you accept Perse school. I was at Trinity Hall on Friday and met one of the Governors. He seemed to think the position of affairs very critical: on the one hand the school is on too low a social scale to catch the sons of the less affluent Dons, and on the other a bran [sic] new City School is on the point of being built within less than a mile. There are some schools which an Archangel cannot make, and this may be one of them.... I know of one good man who reconnoitred and withdrew.[40]

By the following year, pupil numbers had dropped from 213 (the 1900 figure) to 106. In the next eight years, Rouse not only built up numbers in the school, but gave it a national reputation as a centre for progressive methods of teaching which also achieved success in the conventional terms of examinations and scholarships. Here he was assisted, in a way, by the county school's concentration on commercial subjects, since this enabled him to justify making the Perse into what was basically a classical school. The first few years were very difficult: the school's finances were often on the point of collapse and the staff were underpaid. Rouse's best-known appointment was that of Henry Caldwell Cook, famous in his time as the inventor of the 'Play Way'. This was a method which emphasised the pupil's total involvement in drama; though it may well have become popular because of the associations of its title with 'playing', in Cook's hands it was a very serious form of fun.[41] Cook, who was recruited in 1911, had a private income; he was at first paid out of Rouse's pocket, but after two years refused a salary, and in addition paid for the equipping of the school drama room – the 'Mummery'. Sir James Frazer's formidable French wife Lilly paid the salary of Leon Chouville, one of the modern language staff.

By 1906, the school's finances were in a parlous state. In February of that year, A.I. Tillyard, the chairman of the governing body, wrote to Rouse:

> The sub-committee of the Governors met on Friday to frame the estimates. A most serious state of affairs was disclosed. The overdraft at the Bank on December 31 was £1130, and that with £400 of unpaid bills. The estimates show a deficiency of over £1000 on next year's working. We are within measurable distance of two things – the refusal of the Bank to cash any more cheques and the resignation of the governors in a body.[42]

Luckily for Rouse, at least some of his governors recognised that something more than financial viability was at stake. In the same letter, one of them is quoted as saying that 'Your experiment is being watched all over England'; and Tillyard adds, 'It would be a thousand pities to see it collapse now it has got so far.'

What was Rouse's 'experiment'? It was centred on the Direct Method teaching of languages, ancient and modern. But this was only one element, though the one closest to Rouse's heart, in a wide-ranging reform of the curriculum as a whole, which drew on two contemporary ideological currents more commonly found in tension or even opposition: progressivism and efficiency.[43] Rouse's claim for Direct Method teaching was that it was not only more effective than conventional methods in producing linguistic proficiency, but also morally superior as an educational experience. His career at Bedford, Cheltenham and Rugby had left him disillusioned with the traditional methods of grammatical drill:

> After a few years spent as a Schoolmaster, I felt a conviction that there was something radically wrong.... The trouble lay not in the machinery of instruction...[but] in the spirit of the boys. They would work out of a sense of duty, or to please a master whom they liked, or to get promotion...but the work in itself was distasteful.... With the majority of boys, the work was an unmitigated grind, disliked and when possible evaded...why this was so, I did not know...the

whole thing was dead. I had only a feeling that the key to the situation laying in making the work real by some means, and conversation suggested itself as a possible means.[44]

The Direct Method developed by Rouse and his colleagues sought to resurrect the corpse of Classics by changing 'the spirit of the boys'. The elementary paradigms of language were learnt through involvement in dialogue, accompanied by activity. As a pupil got up from a seat, walked away from it, returned to it and sat down again, he uttered, and pragmatically learnt, the words *surgo, ambulo, revenio, sedeo*. Second and third persons were learnt in similar fashion:

> A. Surgo
> Chorus (to A, pointing) Surgit.
> (to Master, pointing at A) Surgit.
>
> B and C. Surgimus
> Chorus (to B and C) Surgitis,
> (to Master) Surgunt.[45]

In a memorandum submitted to the Curricula Committee of the Classical Association in January 1906, Rouse spelled out his reasons for basing the teaching of Greek on the spoken word:

1. *It is natural.* Language is the means of communicating between tongue and ear, and written letters are only a means of storing up the material of language…. They bear the same relation to speech as a musical score to the performance.
2. *It is living.* The written word has no means of compelling attention; the spoken word, if well spoken, and if intelligible, commands attention, and creates a lasting impression in proportion to the force of the speaker's character….
3. *It is speedy.* It allows of many times as much practice in a given time.
4. *It is intelligent.* The difference of person, number etc. between master and pupil cause [sic] the response to be, not a parrot echo, but something new made on the spur of the moment.

Although this approach was radically different from the conventional grammar-and-translation method, Rouse was at pains to stress that grammar was not neglected, but was learnt *seriatim*:

Grammar is set to be learnt in the usual way, but only what bears on the texts. At first the texts are selected to illustrate restricted parts of grammar...but, within limits, it matters little what parts of grammar are first taken. The order will be decided by practical usefulness, i.e. common things first, and as few irregularities as possible.[46]

A related emphasis on inductive, sequential learning underlay his conception of the language curriculum as a whole. The ideal was to begin with English; start French at nine; Latin at 11; and Greek at 14; thus avoiding 'mental indigestion'.

How did all this fit in with the rest of the curriculum? Looking back in 1927, Rouse said that 'On my appointment here, I saw the problem as twofold: languages on the one hand, mathematics and natural sciences on the other. Later, it became clear that there was a third problem, the proper use of handwork.'[47] That Rouse was keen to introduce handwork is shown by the collection of catalogues of craft equipment which survives among his papers, along with letters from headmasters to whom he had written for advice on craftwork. It was also very much in tune with his concern to recover the organic relation of hand and eye which he saw as having been discarded in the age of the machine. The curriculum pamphlets produced for the school from about 1910 suggest that natural science was taught experimentally, and that pupils were involved in observation: 'Natural Science begins with the study of natural objects: animals, birds, insects and the visible world generally'. Yet Rouse shared the mental set common among humanists of his generation, in which holism and a concern for balance were rooted in a determined and specific commitment to the humanities. The *moral* potential of a total curriculum had its seat primarily in arts subjects, rather than in mathematics and natural science. This frame of mind is visible in the Secondary School Regulations of 1904, issued by Robert Morant, Permanent Secretary at the Board of Education, whose support for the Perse was to prove crucial. Science teaching had been expanding in the 1890s in response to the generous grants offered by the Department of Science and Art, to the alarm of the (largely classically-educated) senior officials of the Education Office. When the two bodies were merged into the new Board of Education, Morant was able to equalise the level of grant for arts and science subjects, thus (as he put it) 'correcting a distortion' in the curriculum. Anticipating the change in his report to the school governors in August 1904, Rouse declared that

I believe that no part of the work has been forced at the expense of the rest. Natural Science is a possible exception, but for that we are not responsible; and if there has been undue favour shown to this subject in accordance with the requirements of the Board of Education, the new Regulations of the Board will enable us to remedy this defect in the coming year.[48]

A progressive classical school:
Rouse at the Perse (1907-10)

By 1907, the school was on the way out of its financial crisis. In his report of August 1906, Rouse had emphasised that 'The past year was a crisis in the history of the school', but had added that 'our work is rapidly becoming known in the country. The number of boarders, which has risen from eight at my last report to over thirty, shows this growing appreciation'. In July 1906, a public meeting had been held at the Cambridge Guildhall in support of the school. S.H. Butcher, well known not only as a Greek scholar but also, at the time, as MP for Cambridge University, delivered an encomium on Rouse and his work:

> The school had reached a moment which was the most interesting, but also the most critical, in its whole history. It had a Headmaster, a man of far-reaching and courageous views, who saw his way clearly, who had inspired others, and who had won their confidence. Nothing was wanted except the money....[49]

When the money appeared, it came from a source whose support had special significance. In July 1905, Rouse had appealed direct to Morant for financial support, and had received an encouraging answer:

> ...we had your kind of work particularly in view in framing Section 13[b] of the new Regulations...and we have every hope that under it the Perse School will secure a substantial increase of financial aid from us.[50]

The wheels of bureaucracy turned slowly, but in November 1907, Rouse received an official letter telling him that

23

The Board of Education have decided to approve the application of the governors for a special grant under Article 39 of the Regulations for Secondary Schools, and £200 will therefore be allowed...for the purpose of providing an additional classical assistant master in order to permit the continuance of an experiment already initiated in the school of teaching Latin and Greek by the direct method....[51]

This grant, initially for a maximum of five years, was renewed several times, and in fact continued to be paid throughout Rouse's term of office as Headmaster. The delay in awarding the grant may have been due to red tape.[52] On the other hand, some of the Board's Classics HMIs were dubious about Rouse's methods. At the same time, support for Rouse's claim will have been strengthened by the findings of Headlam, by this time Staff Inspector for Secondary Education, who investigated the teaching of Classics in the Reformgymnasien of Frankfurt in 1906.[53] His report, which was published by the Board in 1910, concluded that the Frankfurt experiments, which incorporated Direct Method teaching and had begun in the early 1890s, had in general proved successful. (Karl Reinhardt, the moving spirit in the Frankfurt reforms, later visited the Perse, and wrote in support of Rouse's work.)

One of the conditions attached to the Board's grant was that some account of the teaching it supported should be published. Rouse and his colleagues W.H.S. Jones and R.B. Appleton accordingly produced two separate pamphlets, one each on Latin and Greek, published in 1910 and 1914 respectively.[54] Both pamphlets combine a certain amount of propaganda for the Direct Method with a remarkably detailed account of its application. This must have entailed a large amount of record-keeping, and indeed some of the forms used for this still survive. Rouse himself was notoriously – and at times wilfully – inefficient in such matters, and Headlam's papers indicate that this aspect of the operation was enforced from the Board's end. The report on Greek is particularly detailed: for example, an appendix of 28 pages is devoted to the development of a Greek vocabulary. Here Rouse gives an alphabetical list of about 1600 words, annotated to show the points in a two-year period at which each of five pupils first used each word. The Greek pamphlet is more than three times as long as the Latin; the comparison indicates where Rouse's primary interest lay.

What kind of classical course is revealed in these pamphlets? Latin was started at the age of 11 or 12, Greek two years later. Conversation in the language taught was the rule from the very beginning. (Here Jones, who carried most of the lower-school teaching, seems to have been more willing than Rouse was to use English explanations. Rouse's teaching was concentrated on the top two forms, where the pupils would have been more fluent in Latin and Greek.)[55] Points of grammar were discussed as they were encountered; this was probably a fairly predictable process, since most of the course books used in the early years were written by Rouse or one of his colleagues, and were designed to introduce a graded variety of grammatical and syntactical points. The pamphlet published by the Board of Education in 1910 includes statistics of test scores which show generally high levels of achievement in composition and translation in the sixth form. The exceptions, as Rouse is careful to point out, are not to be blamed on the Perse:

> Of the 22 boys in question...six came from other schools at the age of 13 to 15. All six, without exception, were in a most lamentable state when they came. Having learnt Latin for four or five years, they were unable to take their place with boys who had been learning for two or three years, and they were hopelessly outclassed even in syntax and accidence: they had no literary conscience, took no pride in being right, wrote nonsense with contentment, and expected generally to be wrong.[56]

The same pattern can be seen in the teaching of Greek. Pupils began at about the age of 14. In the first year they read two books written by Rouse: his *First Greek Course*, which included sufficient grammar and syntax for the year, then his *Greek Boy at Home*, a book of linked synthetic passages of graded difficulty. At the end of the year, grammar was revised in its logical order, rather than in the order in which it had been picked up. In the second year, extracts from Thucydides were read, and a few Platonic dialogues; in the last term, Homer or Herodotus. Throughout the course, the basic activities were reading aloud, followed by question and answer in Greek, the questions designed to bring out the meaning of the text.

Rouse always regarded the advanced work of the sixth form as the crowning achievement of the Direct Method. Here, more than anywhere else, his utopian vision came alive, as in a dusty schoolroom in England, ancient Greece was, in a sense, recreated. In the relevant section of his Board of Education pamphlet, he waxes lyrical, while despairing of being able to transmit the fleeting beauties of the spoken word to the dull permanence of print:

> It is impossible to realise, without having heard it, how wide is the range of the pupils' spoken language.... I wish I could show it here

> as it is; but it is one of those things that pass like a flash and are gone, leaving behind only the impression of pleasure and admiration.... So I give my specimens, reminding readers that they are but the merest scraps, flotsam cast up by the waves, gleanings of the harvest.[57]

These 'gleanings' were jotted down in notebooks, and by the time Rouse retired in 1928, he had recorded several thousand notes of conversation, rejoinders, apt quotations and the like. A selection was published in 1935 under the title *Scenes from Sixth Form Life*. It has ten short chapters, each giving the 'script' of a classroom discussion on a literary passage. Six are Latin (from Virgil, Livy, Cicero and Horace), four Greek (from Thucydides, Aeschylus and Sophocles), the balance probably reflecting the nature of the estimated audience rather than the author's own preference. In his Preface, Rouse explains that he sent copies of the scenes to several of those who had taken part in them, and established that his texts were reasonably accurate; he concludes that 'The impression...is quite truthful, although I cannot say everything was said in those exact words'. One of those who wrote to him after publication, however, denied that sixth-formers could have reached the level implied in the text of the book, and accused Rouse of making it all up. Rouse immediately contacted several of his ex-pupils and asked them for signed statements, which he then forwarded to his assailant, who was not to be persuaded. However, those who took part in the teaching which the book records, are agreed that it does give an accurate picture of what went on in Rouse's sixth-form room; some are able to ascribe particular witticisms to the boys who produced them.[58]

Rouse's Preface also tells us that the classroom he used, and which was also his office, contained a large set of plain texts, to which reference was made by master and boys alike. This picture is confirmed and amplified by P.J. Copping's recollections of being interviewed by Rouse in 1914 for entrance to the school.

> I found myself in a plain class-room, no study, with the whole back wall covered with book-cases well filled, a large master's desk completely covered with brownish-orange volumes so placed as to show the back-titles uppermost, more books on other walls, a map of Greece above the fire-place, and a black-board and easel on which were inscribed characters which I only guessed to be Greek, while in the corner by the window stood what must be Dr. Rouse.
>
> He was a short man, a very short man, no more than 5 ft or 5ft 1 ins, a rounded, plump, tubby man too, with a beard almost as voluminous

as the rest of his head...he...asked me to read from a volume of Milton and one of Macaulay.[59]

Rouse's use of reading out loud as a test is characteristic of his stress on the living word. The life of his classroom lay in the interaction between the rows of original texts (the 'brownish-orange volumes' refers to the early binding style of Oxford Classical Texts) and the verbal interchanges between master and pupils. Rouse stressed the importance of this direct contact with the text: 'the boys always used plain texts, and had no notes at all, except what I gave them, or what they found for themselves; and if I gave them a reference, they had to look it up and copy it for themselves. In revising for examination, they were allowed notes or anything they liked...but for work, plain texts only were used.... Their home work was to revise the day's lesson, and in the first two years of the Sixth form, to write a page of summary in Latin or in Greek.'[60]

For his pupils, it must have been a stimulating but at times nerve-wracking experience to be kept on their toes in the way the *Scenes* suggest. This was especially true for new members of the sixth form, since they were expected to join in with their seniors (at one time, Rouse apparently had pupils who were in their fourth year in the sixth form). Inevitably, the more experienced boys took the lead in verbal challenge and response at first, but the reports of ex-pupils suggest that their juniors were pulled into the debates by the sheer momentum of the conversational crossfire.[61]

The sixth form was the arena where Rouse used language to resurrect the ancient world. No wonder he saw *Scenes* as his finest achievement. Its late appearance is also characteristic; even in the case of a faithful record of the 'living word' in action, Rouse was reluctant to commit this life to the passivity of print. For many years, he resisted requests to write a textbook of his method; the course book *Latin on the Direct Method*, which he wrote with his colleague Appleton, appeared only in 1925.[62] He preferred to have enquirers and sceptics visit the Perse to see the method in operation. His annual reports to the school governors list the increasing number of visitors, from Britain, Europe and beyond, who came to test his claims. Morant sent his HMIs to watch; Reinhardt, whose successes at Frankfurt had led to his promotion to the Prussian Ministry of Education, added his seal of approval; Peter Sokoloff, the travelling inspector of the Russian Imperial education office, made a special trip to England to visit the Perse. By 1910, Rouse had become a public figure in both educational and wider circles. In order to understand the varying reactions to his ideas – on teaching method, on classics and on education more generally – we need to consider his involvement in these wider circles.

The 1902 Education Act and the defence of the Classics

The Act which first established a coherent national system of secondary education in England was passing through Parliament as Rouse began his long term of office at the Perse. Its enactment marked a stage in the transition to state intervention in English education: a transition which took place well after similar events on the continent, and amid accusations that an English tradition of individual freedom and local autonomy had been breached. In the late Victorian decades, the ideology of freedom had buttressed the expansion of the public schools, whose consolidation as an institutional sector in the 1870s had its origins in the rejection of interventionist clauses in the 1869 Endowed Schools Bill. By 1900, the public schools had become established as one of the glories of England: the nurseries of fair play, manliness and Empire. Welded together by a hierarchy of sporting esteem, supported by newly-created school ties, songs and old boys' associations, their self-image was disseminated to a wider world through the public-school novels which proliferated from the 1880s onwards.

In the public-school curriculum, Classics predominated in 1900 almost as it had in the 1860s, when its traditional justifications had been mercilessly dissected by Henry Sidgwick and his fellow-contributors in *Essays on a liberal education*.[63] While public attention, and to a large extent the interest of staff and pupils, was focused on the games field, Classics continued to fill about 40% of the classroom time of the 13-year-old public schoolboy, rising to about 60% two years later. The reasons for its continued dominance had much to do with class and status. In the hierarchies of esteem confirmed and clarified by the great educational commissions of the 1860s – Newcastle, Clarendon and Taunton – the public schools were supreme.[64] New middle-class groups in a socially fluid situation, concerned to confirm or raise their social status, patronised feepaying schools to emphasise their superiority to the families whose children attended the free elementary schools set up by Forster's Education Act of 1870. Distracted from the classroom by the glories of the games field, basking in the admiration of English and foreign observers, the public schools had no reason to change. Some of the more liberal and adventurous schools certainly tried: the introduction of a 'Modern Side' at Harrow, set up explicitly to have equal standing with the 'Classical Side' of the school, is a notable example. But in most of the schools, for most of the pupils, the learning of Classics meant the 'grammar grind' (believed by its supporters, still in a majority in public-school staffs, to make boys into men), followed by the memorising of passages from Horace or Virgil. For a minority, the 'grind' led easily into an invigorating immersion in a wide range of classical texts which were drawn on casually in conversation. For the rump, the best they could hope for was a few half-remembered classical tags which served to demonstrate that they had been to a public school.[65]

Lack of internal reform, however, had increased external pressure for change, which by the 1900s had been powerfully reinforced by a variety of economic and other factors. The agricultural depression of the 1880s; the decelerating expansion of a mature industrial economy; increased competition from Germany and the USA; isolation from Europe, and the threat of Prussian militarism; the degenerationist alarms stemming from evidence of physical and military failure in the Boer War campaigns; the enfranchisement of a working class which might become an ochlocracy: all these factors combined to generate a wave of criticism directed at the public schools. The world had changed, yet the teaching of modern languages and natural science, for example, had made very few inroads into the public-school curriculum. The continuing dominance of Classics thus became a central target for the critics of the schools in the public debates on 'education and the nation' which followed the passage of the 1902 Act.

While the Act was still going through parliament, J.P. Postgate of Trinity College, Cambridge issued a rallying call to the supporters of Classics in the columns of the *Fortnightly Review*.

> At a time when we appear to be on the eve of extensive reconstruction in the higher education system of the country, the first duty of those who believe that a due recognition of the claims of Greek and Latin is vital to our intellectual welfare is to know what they want. It is clear that the Classics will not be allowed the lion's share which has been theirs in the past, and the question is, how much we must struggle to retain.[66]

The publication of Postgate's article led to the foundation, in December 1903, of the CA of England and Wales. Much of its early activity was located on the Cambridge–London axis (Oxford being regarded for several years as a *pays de mission*), so that Rouse was close to the centre of things. In addition, Postgate, who knew Rouse from their attendance at meetings of the Cambridge Philological Society in the 1880s, shared his views on Direct Method. He even forced his own children to ask for food in Latin; if they could not think of the word, they were not given the food. (In her autobiography, his daughter Margaret remembered being refused a sausage when she failed to produce the Latin word for it; she was eventually allowed half a sausage after offering *dimidium*.)[67] Rouse was clearly a candidate for recruitment: energetic, hardworking, both scholar and schoolmaster, his organisational talents and efficiency in publicising a cause evidenced by his work as secretary of the Assistant Masters' Association. He was co-opted onto the Council of the CA in its first year, and remained there for several years. Yet he seems not to have consolidated his position in the Association. Here, as in other fields, his irruption onto the scene produced a favourable initial impact which was not afterwards sustained. Rouse was a man with a vision: by 1903, he had worked out to his own satisfaction what needed to be done to reform English education, and how to do it. This did not make him an easy colleague for those who did not share his vision.[68]

As editor of the CA's publication *The Year's Work in Classical Studies* for its first five issues, Rouse caused some embarrassment by contributing an opening chapter to each issue in which developments in school Classics were reported in forthright terms, and the Direct Method given prominence. (As we shall see, his later editorship of the *Classical Review* was similarly controversial.) Nevertheless, Rouse's views, and his achievements at the Perse, made a considerable impact on his fellow classical teachers; and this was because his proposed reforms seemed to offer a solution to what was otherwise an intractable problem. While they involved a radical alteration of method, their stress on the creation of Latin and Greek was consonant with the English tradition of composition as an educational tool. In this, as in many other things, Rouse was a very conservative radical. In addition, and crucially, he claimed that the Direct Method produced results comparable with those of traditional teaching in about a third of the time. To those who believed that they were about to be forced to surrender 'the lion's share which has been ours in the past', this was welcome news. By 1910, Rouse was able to claim that his small school had won more open scholarships in Classics than had many of the large public schools. This was the basis of the claim made in more detail in the two pamphlets published by the Board of Education: quite simply, the method *worked*.

The CA held off from any public support for Rouse's reforms. Its membership constituted a defensive alliance dominated by dons, public-school masters and country gentlemen. Opinions on the central issues of reform varied widely both within and between these groups: most notably on the contentious question of Compulsory Greek at Oxford and Cambridge, which had dragged on since 1870, and was not settled until after the Great War. Here any public stand would have split the Association in two, and so discussion was, whenever possible, simply avoided. Rouse, on the other hand, was a fierce advocate of the retention of Compulsory Greek, and in fact acted as Secretary to the Cambridge 'Greek Defence Committee'. Conditions were thus ripe for a parting of the ways, and this probably occurred in 1911, when Rouse became involved in the planning of his first summer school.

The Headmasters' Conference, to which Rouse was elected when he was appointed to the Perse, had also been founded as a defensive alliance, and indeed shared some of the CA's characteristics. It was less shy than the CA was of public pronouncements on matters of educational policy; but this was largely because the motions passed at its meetings, however impressive the majority, were not binding on members. At the 1906 Conference, Rouse's old chief James of Rugby 'with characteristic incisiveness commanded us all to use the new pronunciation of Latin, and with equal independence added, "But I'm not going to use it myself".'[69] On his first appearance, at the 1902 conference, Rouse made a vigorous and effective speech whose content strikingly anticipates some of Morant's later policy decisions. He complained that the Board of Education's staff was inadequate to supervise secondary education, especially in the humanities. Of its 15 Chief Inspectors, 14 Inspectors and 29 juniors, not one had been appointed on the strength of general culture or distinction in modern or ancient languages. The information given in *Whitaker's Almanac* suggested that the only one competent to inspect these was Headlam, who was listed as a junior inspector, appointed for a year at a time. Rouse ended by calling for a Treasury grant to cover the whole curriculum, rather than 'science and art' alone, as was then the case.[70]

Not only did Morant introduce a comprehensive grant system under the 1904 Secondary Regulations; he also set up a post whose informal description seems to have been just what Rouse would have wished. In November 1903, his friend W.G. Rushbrooke, Headmaster of St Olave's, wrote to him:

I have been in communication with Morant as to his want of a Chief Inspector for Secondary Schools. I understand that such a man, though nominally under W. Bruce [Morant's second-in-command], would be directly in contact with Morant, and practically an independent official with an army of inspectors under him. They want a man of tact and character, as well as of Academic distinction, who would get on with people, and one who knows enough science not to be fooled by the South. Ken. lot. [i.e., the staff of the former Department of Science and Art, recently merged into the Board of

Education] One whose work it would be to support the literary side of the grammar schools & prevent Borough Councils and S.K. from working their wicked will.
I have ventured to write very strongly in favour of you.[71]

There is no evidence that Rouse was seriously considered for the post. Neither his scientific knowledge nor his tact would have proved equal to the task. This latter weakness became clearer to his colleagues in the HMC as the years passed. Even his major ally in the defence of Greek at their meetings, J.H.E. Crees of the Crypt School, Gloucester, found Rouse's missionary zeal hard to take. Crees later wrote of him:

> The coryphaeus of all Classical linguists is Dr Rouse of Cambridge. He is passionately convinced that there is only one way of teaching the Classics, and many a letter to the papers is an evidence of his zeal.... King Charles's head has a terrible habit of appearing in every composition that the Doctor puts his hand to, and his zeal for his doctrines knows no measure. He is the exact antithesis of the normal Headmaster of a Public School, with his careful attention to convention, his suspicion of novelty, and sometimes his lack of keenness as to anything. In spite of his undoubted ability and remarkable energy, there is not infrequently a soupçon of the ludicrous about his propaganda. What opponent would not be disarmed by such transparent guilelessness, who must not smile at the earnestness and simplicity which no gleam of humour ever relieves, who cannot admire the enthusiasm with which he flings himself into every matter which claims his interest, from the cause of all causes to Handwork or the Scouting Movement?[72]

By 1907, Rouse's single-minded zeal had brought predictable results in the HMC: he was, in effect, provoked into wheeling out his known opinions as the basis for discussion. At the Conference that year, W.H. Flecker of Cheltenham proposed a motion that 'the teaching of Latin and Greek should not aim at getting boys to speak those languages.' He explained that this was 'a personal motion, since they all knew who was the greatest champion of getting boys to speak Latin and Greek. His friend Dr Rouse, whom he respected greatly.' After he had spoken for the motion and Rouse against it, the chairman persuaded Flecker to withdraw the motion, since it had achieved its aim of 'drawing' Rouse.[73]

In such public settings, Rouse seems often to have outworn an initial welcome. The pattern recurs in the CA and in the HMC, where the unconverted remained unconverted and grew irritated. Within the boundaries of the world governed by his vision, he appeared in a rather different light. As a headmaster, he treated his staff as colleagues rather than as subordinates. His own role he saw as essentially that of a co-ordinating teacher. His use of the sixth-form room rather than a headmaster's study reflected the lack of an authoritarian hierarchy in the school (and, incidentally, helps to account for his well-known inefficiency in form-filling). The tributes paid by ex-pupils after his death make it clear that he was a captivating teacher, whose innate dignity allowed him to act in ways which offended conventional notions of etiquette. His habit of visiting classrooms and singing ditties is a case in point. A short, stout figure, he 'walked with short, shuffling steps...yet with a peculiar majesty'.[74] One of his testimonials ends with this declaration: 'everyone who knows him personally recognises in him a certain nobility of personal character.'[75] A testimonial of a more informal kind is preserved among Rouse's papers, in an envelope on which he has written 'Written by Bayles in Horace lesson 1923. Instructive as to what goes on in a dull mind. Character of me.' The envelope contains a small piece of paper on which a childish hand has written

> Horatius Epodon Liber. This is dreadfully boring, Sum Collapsus = I am bored. The headmaster, Dr Rouse: a fat, tubby, cheerful 'old man'. A temper when disturbed, or during bad weather, which precipitates a cold. On the whole, a decent old man. Rarely exceeds himself. Has sent me into the big hall once for not doing his homework. Well, I don't blame him. I'd have done the same myself if I'd been in his place. Can be both nasty and kind. Gives good advice except as regards Classics, of which he is the summmum bonum.'[76]

Champion of the Classics

In the second half of the Edwardian decade, as Rouse's work at the Perse became more widely known, he emerged as a leading public defender of classical education against its detractors. Unfettered by the diplomatic considerations which constrained the spokesmen of the CA, he brought to his public utterances both an unusual range of experience and an unusual willingness to employ it in argument. Thus his accounts of the Perse's achievements often began with an attack on the iniquities of the scholarship system – an area with which he had become familiar while Secretary of the Assistant Masters' Association in the1890s. In a paper published in 1908, he pointed out that in the previous year, 271 scholarships and exhibitions in Classics had been awarded at Oxford and Cambridge. Of these, the 'seven leading schools' (Winchester, Eton, Harrow, Rugby, Shrewsbury, Charterhouse, Westminster) had won 50, while the seven leading day schools had gained 53. Rouse lists all the advantages of wealth and staffing possessed by the first group of schools, and argues that 'With all these advantages, they ought to sweep everything before them.... Yet Eton and Harrow...stand third on the list of the seven...'.[77]

Rouse's position in relation to the prestigious public schools was rather like that of Edward Thring forty years before: the initiative in education, he claimed, was passing to less famous but more enlightened schools, who not only did better in the scholarship stakes, but also took better care of 'the average boy'. From this point of view, Eton constituted an obvious target; and so it must have been particularly galling for Rouse to read the attacks on the classical curriculum published by A.C. Benson. Benson had recently left Eton for Magdalene College, Cambridge, and having begun by believing in the centrality of Classics to education, had been disillusioned by the weekly Etonian round of mechanically-composed verses. Classical education, he declared, was 'a kind of intellectual nihilism' which led nowhere and made most boys dull. 'At present the classical training seems to me too often to be a sort of topiary art – the carving of yew-trees into peacocks and cubes; whereas education ought to be a kind of forestry, giving each tree the full advantages of congenial soil and water and room to grow'.[78] Benson's agricultural imagery belongs to a long English tradition which had previously been invoked, for example, by Edward Copleston in his *Replies to the calumnies of the Edinburgh Review against Oxford* in 1810-11, where the 'Platonic reverie' of French education is likened to the espaliered hedge of the French garden, and contrasted, in the manner of Edmund Burke, with the freedom of the English oak tree. Rouse replied in the same ideological terms, by presenting himself as a down-to-earth pragmatist. Benson, he declared, was a man of rarefied views, like one observing from an aeroplane. Rouse himself, on the other hand, resembled Sisyphus, toiling up a hill in a land of plain facts. Benson's ideas were speculative, Rouse's had been proved in practice.[79]

The Copernicus of classical education? (1910-14)

In 1910, the 'Great Experiment' was put on a new and more secure footing when Rouse bought five acres of land in Cherry Hinton, then on the outskirts of Cambridge. Here he built a school house for himself and for boarders. Several features of this step deserve to be emphasised, quite apart from the commitment to the experiment which it represented. In the first place, it reminds us how much of what the Perse achieved was made possible by the financial support of private individuals. Rouse told the Governors in 1913 that two of his staff had been working without salary; and in his retrospective statement of 1927, that Henry Caldwell Cook, appointed in 1911, had been paid out of Rouse's own pocket at first, and had then worked for nothing for ten years.[80] How could Rouse afford to buy five acres of land and build a house on it? His income from capitation fees will have risen as numbers increased in the school, but a more important factor was his inheritance from his father, who died in 1909.[81] Since his sister Alice, who kept house for him until her death in 1939, was already living with him, anything she inherited would presumably have been available for their shared accommodation.

Cook, as we have already seen, used his private income not only to work for several years without salary, but also to equip 'The Mummery', the drama room where he practised his 'Play Way' English teaching. The financial help provided by Lilly Frazer has also been mentioned. A more unlikely benefactor was Benson, whose disputes with Rouse on the value of classical education have been described earlier. By 1916, however, Benson had become a strong supporter of the Perse, to the extent of making up salary cuts out of his own pocket. He had become a governor in 1911, and liked the atmosphere of the place, which he found relaxed and liberal. Rouse himself was more difficult to take, but Benson admitted that he was a fine teacher. Rouse's recurrent appeals to the governors for money are described in Benson's voluminous diaries as 'insolent'; and when Rouse added himself to a group being photographed at the investiture of James Loeb with an honorary degree, Benson denounced him in his diary as 'a nasty little toad'.[82]

The move to Cherry Hinton represented the realisation of a utopian vision which underpinned both Rouse's advocacy of Direct Method and his proposals for curricular reform. This is thus an appropriate point at which to try to describe its nature, its origins and the sources on which Rouse drew in realising it.

Fig. 2 Rouse the horseman, by D.C. Bolton. [Perse School Archives]

The living word: a mission of social renewal

The utopian vision which Rouse hoped to realise at Cherry Hinton Glebe had many ramifications and a variety of sources. It drew on the romantic and ruralist views of John Ruskin and William Morris, while rejecting Morris' socialism. The Burkean glorification of 'little England' to be found in G.K. Chesterton was another influence. Cecil Sharp's recovery of disappearing folk songs and dances in a countryside which was losing its population to the cities was also a task close to Rouse's heart; he himself often engaged the older inhabitants of Cambridgeshire villages in conversation, noting down both the tales they told and dialectal peculiarities in their speech. Some of this recording was carried out during what he called 'Rouse's rural rides' – horseback tours of East Anglia which he made in holidays between 1911 and 1932, and which are summarised in one of his travel notebooks. His correspondence with the Oxford classical scholar, Mozartean and ornithologist William Warde Fowler also indicates that Rouse habitually rode across country when he visited Fowler's house in the Oxfordshire village of Kingham. (Some of Fowler's letters include a jocular greeting to his friend's chestnut mare Kitty.)[83] Rouse's vision also drew on a love for Homeric Greece which is evident both in the translations of Homer he published in the 1930s, and in his several Aegean journeys around the turn of the century, when he sailed in the wake of Ulysses. In English history, his favourite period, predictably, was the Elizabethan era, when those later heroes Drake, Frobisher and Hawkins sailed the seas; an age which also produced many fine translations of classical authors, some of which Rouse edited for republication in collaboration with Israel Gollancz, a ' nd from his college days.[84] Similarly, in the Greece and England of his own day he felt at home in the country, where the organic unity of ancient ways remained uncorrupted by modernity. Here the small world of the Perse offered a way to resist this corruption by what Rouse saw as building on the public-school tradition in a new way: 'The problem of this century', he said 'is, how to create such a type of...school, as will assimilate what is best in the national tradition amidst the alien influence of industrial life.'[85] And here we reach the heart of his vision: a simple yet powerful impulse characteristic of Edwardian thinkers and writers, the concern to assert the value of human life against the deadening effects of industrialisation and urbanisation, bureaucracy and the machine. This Edwardian pattern of belief is very well summed up by Richard Ellmann in his essay 'Two faces of Edward'. He points out that Edwardian literature tended to be secular, yet earnest. Where religion had in the late Victorian period been rejected (as by W.B. Yeats, Edmund Gosse and Samuel Butler, for example), now it was used, but as a metaphor. What was capitalised now was not God, but Life. For the writers of the 1900s, the transcendent was immanent in the earthy, and 'the central miracle for the Edwardian is the sudden alteration of the self'.[86]

'The sudden alteration of the self.' That was what the Direct Method offered for Rouse: baptism in the living waters of speech. It is not clear what led to the attenuation of his Baptist faith, but his registration as a *lay* student at Regent's Park College at the end of the 1870s indicates, as has already been suggested, that he was, at the least, not committed to following in his father's footsteps. His proposal to go to China as a missionary clearly had a large cultural and literary component; something which the Baptist emphasis in the Indian mission-field will, of course, have encouraged. By the end of the 1880s, his commitment to Greek literature and to comparative philology had become central components of his outlook on life. Where did this leave his specifically religious belief? Did his love of words take over, or simply fuse with his love of the Word? It is difficult to tell. In a partly autobiographical piece written near the end of his life, he declared, 'I do not really like preaching, although I have done some'.[87] Most revealing, perhaps, is a piece with the characteristic title *Logic and life*, which appeared in a progressive educational journal in 1937. This ends with an attempt 'to show how great literature can impress the hearer with profound truth, which slips in by the way unnoticed, and remains because it was unnoticed, when the hearers might turn deaf ears to a sermon.' Rouse's text is taken from the *Oedipus Coloneus*:

> Oedipus has bidden farewell to the world, and as he sets out on his last journey, he says to the bystanders –
>   Pass on, and touch me not –

> Is this not remarkable coincidence? Does it not recall the words which were spoken four hundred years later, 'Touch me not, for I am not yet ascended unto my Father?'

Then after giving a translation of the scene in which Oedipus disappears from the vision of mortals, Rouse comments

> This final scene is like Elijah soaring to Heaven in his chariot of fire. Both in its grandeur and in its mystery, it transcends the teachings of Greek religion as we know them.... It is the doctrine of the Christian

scriptures shown in a man, not in a sermon; and as coming from
heathen Greece, it may bring comfort if in after life a man's faith is
disturbed by the ferment of speculation. Beside the figure of Oedipus
translated, even Theseus looks small; and all around were amazed, as
that company was amazed who beheld the Ascension of Christ.

Another passage also illustrates the assimilation of Hellenism and Christianity into an essentially ethical vision:

> There are clouds and storms around us, but although clouds and
> darkness are round about the Almighty, yet righteousness and
> judgment are the habitation of his seat. Ours is the first Christian
> civilisation.... All through history...the good is the only thing which
> survives all. When the little world of Greece was threatened by Baal
> in the East and Moloch in the West...Greece won the day. So it will
> be with Christian civilisation.... We cannot love our work...unless
> we build it on the rock of true principles.... Unless there is
> something outside the physical universe, unless there is right and
> wrong, we are the slaves of accident and blind guides to those we
> profess to teach. So they will find as they grow up, and a very strong
> faith in something alone will sustain them.... Why not call this object
> of faith by the name of God?[88]

The physical basis for the moral renewal which Rouse hoped to bring
about in the service of this faith was the new Perse School House which he
built in Cherry Hinton. Its semi-rural setting located it between the urban
world to which he ascribed so many of England's evils, and the countryside, the real England, from whose organic warmth could be drawn the
strength to resist the bleak, mechanical world of the town. It thus constituted, in embryo, a kind of missionary beach-head where the lessons
Rouse had learnt from Ruskin in the 1880s might be put into practice. The
School House had stables nearby, and at one time Rouse even ran a small
farm which supplied milk both to the school and to the local inhabitants.

The school he built up in the first decade of his rule at the Perse was
described in an official booklet published in 1910 in these terms: 'The
Perse School may be described as *a classical school with an all-subject
curriculum*. It aims at being at once liberal and efficient.'[89] If this suggests
that the Perse was halfway between a public school and one of the new
progressive schools, this is because Rouse was trying to turn the classical
curriculum into the vehicle of a progressive education. This may explain
why, despite his involvement in progressivism (he served on the committee

of the New Education Fellowship, spoke at their conferences and contributed to their journal *The New Era*), he and the Perse do not appear in accounts of English progressive education.[90] The ideological basis of his mission is plainly revealed in an unpublished essay of 1912:

> If we compare England in 1912 with England in 1812, we shall be struck with one great difference. In 1812 the life of England was in the country, now it is in the town. Moreover, the country communities were self-supporting to a large extent: they made what they wanted to use. Machines have changed all that. They have...made men's work less intelligent, broken the links between maker, men, and thing used.... In 1812, education was given largely by daily life. The artisan...used his hands, eye, and intelligence together, and took a pride in what he made.... Now all is changed. The 19th century, which is the age of machines, is also the age of books. In the course of it, the middle and upper classes have more and more lost touch with realities.... The lower classes have split into two divisions. One part, ever dwindling, clings to the land.... The other part, much larger, comprises those who live by machines.... The villager is part of a small community...the industrial workers are not.... It is more than 40 years since Mr Forster's Act organised elementary education.... What that act did was, to gather the children together...and to drill them in book knowledge.... Have we not heard the meaningless drone of recited poetry, and seen the rows of children, stiff as so many wooden dolls, learning every day how to talk in a Cockney twang in place of their native dialect?... The future of England depends on what we make of these masses of troubled children.... This means a complete new-modelling of our system....[91]

This 'new-modelling' was reflected in the emphasis on handwork in the school, as well as the training of ear and eye through Direct Method teaching. While still an undergraduate, Rouse had written to the aged Ruskin for advice. The sage had replied, 'Your question is answered by the quotation "I have heard of thee by the hearing of the ear".... Listen as much as you like, see as much as you can, and don't be afraid of doing either.'[92] His interest in handwork also predates his appointment to the Perse; in the 1890s, his friend Peter Giles showed him how to build and operate a loom. After he arrived at the Perse, Rouse wrote off for samples of craft equipment, and sounded out headmasters who had introduced handwork into their curricula. More generally, Rouse's rural antimodernism was evident in his abomination of machinery. The motor car, referred to as the 'hell-waggon', was detested above all. When Rouse arrived at school from the School House, on horse or bicycle, 'he would suddenly dismount and, without looking round, hold up his hand to stop the traffic, which jerked and bounced to a sudden halt. Then he waddled solemnly across.'[93]

The author of the above anecdote was at the Perse in the 1920s, by which time motorised traffic was common enough to constitute a peril for pedestrians and cyclists. Rouse's colleague Postgate was fatally injured when his bicycle collided with a steam lorry in 1926; earlier on, one of the Perse School porters had been killed by a horse-drawn tram just outside the school. But Cambridge's semi-rural university centre, and the proximity of the countryside, still enabled its inhabitants to regard it as a refuge from the wider world of metropolitan bustle. Over thirty years later, Postgate's son Raymond characterised his father's view of the world in the following terms:

> The inner fortress, the citadel…was the study of the Greek and Latin languages…. The civilised world…was also to be found in Oxford and Trinity College, Dublin; Harvard and Yale…. The recognition given to Rome, Athens and Madrid was almost wholly a matter of Christian charity…. Outside this civilised world there existed, but were neither understood nor discussed, what were in effect the wild lands. Here people earned their living by working with their hands, trading, owning property, or engaging in politics…the rule-of-thumb here was to support the party calling itself Conservative, because most changes, for the last half-century anyhow, had harmed rather than helped classical studies.[94]

This view of Cambridge as a bastion of civilisation in a hostile world was not peculiar to Rouse and Postgate. The latter's next-door neighbour, John Maynard Keynes, held the same view, according to his most recent biographer: '…if England was a paradise, Cambridge was a paradise within a paradise, even more remote from the world of practical affairs.'[95] And a view consonant with Postgate's is also evident in Housman's Cambridge inaugural of 1911: 'Our first task is to…acquire…the tastes of the classics; not to come stamping into the library of Apollo on the Palatine without so much as wiping our shoes on the doormat, and cover the floor with the print of feet which have waded through the miry clay of the nineteenth century into the horrible pit of the twentieth.'[96]

A vision and its sources: ancient and modern

The major cultural support for Rouse's mission lay in his love of all things Greek. He had travelled in Greece and the Levant several times in the 1890s, on foot and on horseback, visiting sites and exploring remote areas of the countryside. As he went, he kept an illustrated diary in which were recorded significant encounters, inscriptions and minor architectural gems. Children who gave directions, brought food or were otherwise helpful were rewarded with gifts, often knives and other objects which he had confiscated from his pupils at Cheltenham. One of the things he most enjoyed was the prevalence of the second person singular; he notes with disapproval that the more distant plural forms appear when one approaches the town.[96] Here his rural organicist ideas are fused with his conception of the centrality of speech. The adoption of so-called 'purified' speech as a standard form in Greece infuriated him, representing, as he saw it, the victory of bookish urban intellectuals over the countryman. A letter to the press protesting at this met with a response from D.G. Hogarth, who pointed out that Rouse appeared to equate Greece with its rural areas.[98]

Among Rouse's major concerns while travelling was the collection of folktales. He had joined the Folk-Lore Society in 1891 and served as its President in 1905-6; the society's journal *Folk-Lore* published several pieces of his, on subjects ranging from ancient Greek religion to Indian mythology. Perhaps his largest enterprise in this area was the commissioning of a collection of tales from Jacobos Zarraftis, a Greek from the island of Cos. This corpus was drawn on by R.M. Dawkins for his *Forty-five Tales from the Dodecanese* (Cambridge University Press, 1950); the manuscript originals were bequeathed by Rouse to the library of the Cambridge Classical Faculty. It was presumably during these travels, too, that he acquired the nineteenth-century Greek MSS of spells and charms which he left to Christ's College.[99] In all this activity, one of Rouse's concerns was to trace continuities with classical Greece. The modern Greek spells, for example, can be seen as an extension of the subject matter of his bulky volume on *Greek Votive Offerings*, which the University Press published in 1902. He was widely read in both Greek and Roman authors, but his preferences are fairly clear: Greek rather than Latin, and in Greek, the tragedians, Plato, but especially Homer and Pindar. For Rouse, Homer was at once heroic and down-to-earth; while Pindar's mixture of high-flown grandeur and homely mottoes delighted Rouse as much as (he claimed) they offended some scholars. Discussing Pindar with one of his correspondents in the 1930s, he wrote that the poet composed for both the literate and the ordinary people in his audience – just like Shakespeare.[100]

The Loeb Classical Library

Rouse's wide reading stood him in good stead when he began work as one of the founding editors of James Loeb's 'Classical Library' in 1911. Loeb's original choice had been Frazer, who was tempted, but who turned down the proposal when his publisher, Macmillan, refused to take the Library.[101] One of Frazer's conditions for acceptance had originally been that he should have an assistant editor. Frazer's favoured candidate was Rouse, who was indeed an obvious choice: the editor of several series of English, Latin and Greek texts; well versed in both classical literature and comparative philology; ex-editor of *The Year's Work in Classical Studies* (1906-10), and editor of the *Classical Review* from 1911 to 1920; based in Cambridge, with a foot in the worlds of scholarship and schoolteaching. Rouse's co-editor was his friend Page, who retired from Charterhouse to edit the series. It appears from surviving letters between them that Rouse was asked first (perhaps Frazer suggested Rouse, who then counter-proposed Page). Page wrote to him in January 1911, 'It is very good of you to take second place when you should have been first'.[102] The reason for his doing so is fairly clear: in 1911, Rouse was much busier than Page. Apart from the running of the Perse and his editorial and other writing, he was preparing to launch his first 'School of Latin Teaching', which was held in Bangor, North Wales in September of that year.

The supposition that Rouse was at first regarded as sole or chief editor is strengthened by the fact that he was commissioned to write the publicity booklet for the Library, which carried the characteristic title 'Machines or Mind?' The major characteristic of the booklet is a zealous determination, remarkable even in Rouse, to see nothing but good in the ancients, and nothing but bad in the modern world. Thus Aeschylus is 'the loftiest intellect of all who ever thought on this earth'; Sophocles is 'the perfect artist, who never wastes a word'; Plato is 'the most perfect literary artist in prose of all that ever wrote'. Later on, Rouse remarks that 'Of the classical age, while some of the best has perished, very little remains that is not good.' Similarly with the classical languages themselves: 'Modern English is full of roundabouts, of metaphors without meaning, verbal shams: Greek and Latin are plain, direct, true.' 'Greek...is noble. There is no vulgarity in classical Greek and no affectation.... Latin is usually strict, logical, periodic. Thus these languages help to cure that slovenliness of thought which is a mark of the modern world.'[103] No wonder the *Times Educational Supplement*, which welcomed the first volumes of the Library, was 'less pleased by Dr Rouse's pamphlet "Machines or Mind?"...Dr Rouse's zeal...has outrun his discretion. He sins by over-emphasis.'[104]

'Machines or Mind?' was published in 1912, in advance of the first Loebs, which appeared in the autumn of that year. But it was written in 1911 (Heinemann's office copy is dated the 7th June 1911), and Rouse was presumably working on it in the first half of that year. Its excess of zeal may thus be related to Rouse's current involvement in public debate, this time not with an anti-classical humanist like Benson, but with a more ferocious adversary: the polemical biologist Ray Lankester. Lankester's attack on Classics had appeared in March; Rouse replied soon afterwards in a pamphlet, denouncing all things modern, mechanical and material, and claiming that 'the Greek spirit is the ideal to balance all this stupid materialism'.[105] The extreme tone of Rouse's Loeb pamphlet probably stems from the increasingly polarised debate in which he was engaged when he wrote it.

The Association for the Reform of Latin Teaching

By 1911, Rouse must have felt that his position was consolidated. The Perse was on a firmer financial footing, the School House was in operation, a steady stream of visitors from different parts of the world came to watch his teaching and he had become a minor celebrity through his involvement in educational debate in a variety of spheres. It was at this point that he organised what was to be the first of a series of 'Schools of Latin'. The idea may have come from an invitation he accepted, at about this time, to conduct a summer school at Columbia University in 1912.

The first 'School of Latin' was held at Bangor from 28th August to 11th September. Rouse had connexions there already: E.V. Arnold, the Professor of Latin, had been at Cambridge with him in the early 1880s,[106] while R.L. Archer, the Professor of Education, had examined some of the Perse forms in Latin and had been impressed by the teaching he saw. Arnold was a strong believer in the efficacy of Direct Method, and used it with his students. The staff at Bangor were inclined to be interested in questions of Elementary Method, since their intake consisted largely of farmers' sons and daughters: some with little secondary education, some without English, being monoglot in Welsh.[107] Arnold's nickname at Bangor, in fact, was 'Forum', derived from his introductory Latin reading-book *Forum Romanum*. The School appears to have been a great success. Over a hundred teachers attended: 'the very first time', as the *Times* report commented, 'on which those teachers who agreed with [Rouse and his followers] had been concentrated in one centre for a common purpose.'[108]

Fig. 3 The master and his disciples. A photograph taken at the Exeter Summer School in 1946. The seated figures include those of Rouse's most influential pupils, Cyril Peckett (left) and Frank Lockwood (second from left). [Association for the Reform of Latin Teaching]

The school included demonstration lessons with pupils from local schools, reading groups, lectures on phonetics and conversation practice in Latin and Greek. Postgate, who was now Professor of Latin at Liverpool, came to inspect and to lecture; Arnold wrote short Latin plays which were performed by the participants; and Owen Owen, Chief Inspector of the Central Welsh Board of Examinations, declared that 'the reformed pronunciation of Latin presented little or no difficulty to pupils acquainted with the Welsh language.'[109] A second School, held at Bangor a year later, was also declared a success, though numbers were slightly lower – 91 as compared to 110 the year before. Some of the demonstration classes were provided by Whitgift School, Croydon, where two Classics masters had been converted to the Direct Method (one was a pupil of Rouse's). By now, a degree of organisational continuity had been achieved, and some permanence of purpose is suggested by the changed name of this School: 'School for the Reform of Latin Teaching'. At the large and successful School held in 1913 on Rouse's home ground in Cambridge, which attracted nearly 200 attenders, a general meeting formally set up the Association for the Reform of Latin Teaching (ARLT); a constitution was drawn up; and a subcommittee promptly set to work to assemble an agreed definition of 'Direct Method'. It must already have been apparent that differences of opinion existed as to how much – if any – English was allowable in direct-method Classics. At the first School, W.H.S. Jones, who had for several years carried the bulk of the lower-school teaching at the Perse, insisted that a blanket refusal to use English was simply pedantic. Frank Jones of King Edward VI School, Birmingham declared himself to be a 'half-hogger' in the matter; that is, he compromised between the utopian ideal of total 'directness' and the pedagogic necessity of introducing explanations in English.[110]

By 1914, then, Rouse had consolidated two separate bases for his mission: the Perse and the ARLT. At the School House, he had the opportunity to create a microcosm of the good life with which to resist the evils of modernity and mechanism. An important adjunct to this attempt was the setting up not only of a preparatory department, but even a 'pre-prep' ('my babies' as Rouse called them). This meant that a considerable number of the boys entering the Perse at 11 had been 'prepared' for its 'liberal and efficient' life for five or six years. Again, it is notable that both developments come at about this time: Rouse bought the preparatory school premises in 1910, and started the 'babies' school with his own funds in the following year. As with the School House, the school was to a considerable extent Rouse's kingdom.[111] Yet it has to be asked whether this consolidation did not reflect, at one level, a failure to broadcast his message effectively. In other words, consolidation implied retrenchment. Given Rouse's utopian and antimodernist views, it was perhaps inevitable that he would retreat to a small paradise where life could be as it should be. But the move certainly represents a retreat from the campaign he had waged on a series of fronts since 1902: in the CA, the Headmasters' Conference and in the press. Yet in Rouse's own terms, it was a consistent move, since it followed the logic of his own conviction that change was accomplished by example rather than by ratiocination.[112]

Relations with the CA presented a particular problem. The CA preferred to make its agreed policy known through cautious public statements which were calculated not to offend any of its members. Rouse's new association, by its very existence, challenged both the CA's effective monopoly of the field and its method of proceeding. Rouse's own position as a CA council member and colleague of Postgate, its founder, made the relationship even more delicate. Relations between the two men were already somewhat strained by differences of opinion over the running of the *Classical Review*, which Rouse edited with A.D. Godley of Oxford, and of whose editorial board Postgate was chairman. In December 1913, an anonymous article written by Godley appeared in the *Review* denouncing the new-fangled terminology of modern students of grammar. This led to protests to the editorial board, and Rouse and Godley were instructed to print a reply by Arnold. However, they claimed that his manuscript reached them too late for inclusion in the next issue. The members of the Editorial Board also appear to have been embarrassed by evidence that the two editors, who also acted as secretaries to the Greek Defence Committees in their respective universities, were using their editorial positions to further their campaign against the abolition of Compulsory Greek. Crees, in his thumb-nail sketch of Rouse, in fact declared that his 'devoted worshippers...have contrived to capture the leading Classical organ'.[113] The board struggled to replace the obstreperous editors, but the onset of war did not help, and after refusals from several candidates, they gave up until 1920. In that year Godley resigned, and Rouse was immediately given his notice.[114]

Even before these difficulties, relations had been strained by Rouse's editing of *The Year's Work in Classical Studies* (1906-10). Each issue had opened with a survey of developments in teaching method and curriculum, written by himself from an openly direct-methodist perspective. (After his replacement as editor, this chapter was omitted.) It was along these lines, in fact, that the relationship between the two bodies was diplomatically for-malised. The CA was to deal with 'high policy', the ARLT with questions of method. The first issue of the ARLT's new journal *Latin Teaching* put it like this:

> We are glad to record that great progress has been made in removing the misapprehension that the work of the Association may clash with that of the CA.... In point of fact both the two Associations and their spheres of action are different, and rather complementary than competitive. The CA exists to propagate interest in the greatness of the ancient world and its language [sic]. Our association exists to investigate the minor questions of teaching that language [sic].[115]

Into the sidelines (1914-21)

The defence of Classics in wartime (1914-18)

The outbreak of war in 1914 dealt a heavy blow to Rouse and the ARLT. The summer school planned for September was cancelled: promises of attendance had come from several countries, including Germany. The young men were called up, leaving the infant association few in number and largely female in membership – a situation which was to recur, to its embarrassment, in the postwar years. Tentative moves to establish a working relationship with the CA foundered in the first half of 1914. The larger body held a discussion on the Direct Method, and suggested setting up a committee to pronounce authoritatively on its nature, limits and possibilities. The ARLT not surprisingly backed away from the idea with some speed: an authoritative report was no good to them unless it could be guaranteed to give authoritative *support* for the method. The CA was informed that the proposal was premature; and on suggesting a small-scale preliminary inquiry, was informed that the matter had better wait until the next ARLT summer school could discuss the matter. The school was cancelled, the enquiry never held.[116]

The war interrupted the expansion of Rouse's effort at a crucial point. It also brought out the powerful patriotic (some would say chauvinistic) element in his view of the world. Before the war, he had published a satirical pamphlet entitled *The Sleepers* under the pseudonym *M.P.* This belongs to the current fashion for invasion literature, and explains how an enormous German force, having reached the English coast, is driven off in terror by a distant rumbling sound which they assume comes from defence batteries, but which is in fact the collective snoring of the English nation. The pamphlet also gives vent to Rouse's detestation of politicians and bureaucrats: 'A most extraordinary ministry was formed. At the head of the various departments were placed men who understood the subjects concerned...a distinguished school master at the Board of Education'.[117] The war also led him, as it did many other Englishmen, to hold anti-German views of great virulence. In 1918 he wrote to the publisher John Murray, 'I dislike exceedingly associating my name with German vileness, as I should in touching a German hand...the Germans are false, corrupt, and heart-less...'.[118] After the war, he wrote a short book which combined such feelings with the approach to life through words which formed the basis of his teaching methods. The book is called *Les Allemands peints par eux-mêmes;* it was published by the French firm of Hachette after English publishers refused to take it. An advertising slip describes it as 'a serious, almost tragic and often comic psychological study of the degradation of a nation, as seen and testified to by nearly 1,000 novels...'. There are two illustrations: a portrait of 'fierté Française' (Van Gogh's 'L'Arlésienne') and 'dureté Allemande' (a portrait of Nietzsche). In the text, Rouse seeks to portray different aspects of German life through literature. In the chapter on language, he declares that 'La langage Germanique a toujours quelque chose de grotesque...la langage est sans grâce; il abonde en paroles et choque l'oreille par ses éternelles cadences trochaïques, qui se suivent, six, sept...même neuf à la file'.[119]

Among the consequences of the wartime situation, as it revealed the weakness of Britain's industrial base and scientific and technical educa-tion, was a growing campaign for educational reconstruction. The debates on education stimulated by the activities of the Neglect of Science Com-mittee in 1916 led to the appointment of a series of official committees (on science 1916; modern languages 1916; English 1919; and Classics 1919). The pro-science campaign was led, among others, by the biologist Lankes-ter and by H.G. Wells.[120] Their manifesto, which appeared in *The Times* on February 2nd 1916, pointed to the inadequacy of British industrial produc-tion in meeting the demand for war material, and identified the continued domination of the public-school curriculum by the humanities, especially Classics, as a major culprit. A month later, the Teachers' Guild set up an Education Reform Council, whose remit was 'to consider the condition of Education in England, and to promote such reform-movements as may be necessary.'[121] Rouse had been President of the Guild in 1912, and was asked to join the new Council's committees on Curricula and on Examin-ations. The result was a pamphlet, published in 1917, whose section on Latin and Greek betrays the compromises and accommodations Rouse must have been forced to make with the more traditionally-minded mem-bers of his committee. Thus the importance of reading aloud is stressed – 'The work *at first* [my emphasis] will be largely oral', but Compulsory Greek, in effect, denounced: 'That a smattering of Greek should be a *sine qua non* for admission to Oxford and Cambridge is an anomaly that will justly be swept away.'[122] This can hardly have pleased Rouse, who as secretary of the Greek Defence Committee at Cambridge was committed to fighting the abolition of Compulsory Greek to the last ditch.

For the most part, however, these debates had moved onto a rarefied establishment terrain where Rouse had little purchase. Subject associations in the sciences and humanities met in some haste under the auspices of the Royal Society and the British Academy respectively; while their leading figures took part in discussions with Lankester and the Neglect of Science Committee. Later in 1916, the government set up committees to investigate the position of sciences and modern languages in the educational system. In the following year, the classicists moved to regain the initiative, and a weighty deputation led by Viscount Bryce called on the Board of Education, which agreed to set up a similar committee on the position of Classics. The committee, which was chaired by the Marquess of Crewe, was appointed in 1919 and reported in 1921. The published report provided a valuable collection of both statistical information and opinion. As far as the latter is concerned, the reader is obliged to read between the lines of measured prose. Fortunately, although the papers of the committee are not held by the Public Record Office – they were probably destroyed in the second War – a full set is preserved among the papers of Gilbert Murray, who was a member of the committee and attended almost all its meetings.[123]

The Committee sent three of its members to inspect the Perse, and took evidence from Rouse and his colleague Appleton. They also heard comments on Direct Method teaching in the evidence of other witnesses. The representatives of the Incorporated Association of Assistant Masters claimed that 'Few teachers speak in favour of the "Direct Method" as applied to Latin. In Kent, one boys', two girls' schools use it; two boys', four girls' schools a modification of it; fourteen boys', nine girls' schools condemn it…nearly all the teachers who condemn it have tried it and found it unsatisfactory.'[124] Two of Rouse's former colleagues appeared to have recanted, at least in part: Postgate declared that 'Direct Method secures reality but sometimes at the expense of accuracy, that is, truth', while Arnold described it as 'a useful auxiliary, but slow, and does not provide adequately for the study of form.'[125] The transcript of the Committee's interview with Rouse conveys an air of somewhat tired courtesy. King Charles' Head had been brought out too often, and everyone knew Rouse's views. Thus the questions addressed to him seem peripheral and trivial; for example, 'How did he come to be interested in Direct Method?'[126]

The Committee's report, in Rouse's words, 'praised us with faint damns'. While acknowledging the valuable influence of his work in bringing the importance of oral work to the attention of teachers, the Committee concluded that the Direct Method was not suitable for general adoption. It worked impressively in the hands of skilled and scholarly teachers, but required a greater knowledge of language than was possessed by the average secondary school teacher. In addition, it gave up the benefits of translation into English, and made it impossible to comment in detail on a text as it was being read.[127]

This marginalising of the ARLT's views was accompanied by a parallel decline in the Association's influence. After the war, the Board of Education began to organise its own summer schools; an offer from the ARLT to run them for the Board was declined. At the Board's school, L.W.P. Lewis of Bradford Grammar School gave a series of lectures on Latin teaching in which he politely but firmly ruled out the Direct Method: 'I do not believe in the direct method for Latin'.[128] The Board, one may infer, had decided that the monopoly of discussions of teaching method by the proponents of the Direct Method was unfortunate. And monopoly, up to then, it had been. If one looks at the teachers' handbooks, encyclopedias, articles in educational journals and so on for the first two decades of the century, one finds that the treatment of Classics is almost without exception by Rouse or by one of his followers: Jones, F.R. Dale, Appleton *et al.*

By 1921, the ARLT's monopoly on advice to teachers was gone, and its influence much diminished. In addition the end of the War had found 'a sadly weakened leadership and a moribund Society', as the editor of *Latin Teaching* admitted in 1921.[129] By that time, however, membership had risen from 70 in 1918 to over 200. Successful summer schools had been organised, and that of 1921, at Cambridge, had 'rivalled in interest and enthusiasm that of 1913'.[130] Rouse and his followers marched into the 1920s rebuffed but unbowed.

Last years at the Perse (1922-8)

In 1922 the Board of Education carried out a full inspection of the school. In Rouse's period of office, there had been two previous inspections. In 1904, the HMIs had stressed his qualifications, experience, energy and teaching abilities, but had added, 'He teaches all the time...this is too much...he needs time to supervise other masters.' The concentration on Classics also worried them: 'No system can be considered permanently satisfactory which involves the treatment of boys who do not specialise in Classics as outside the normal school course.' They were clearly impressed by the 'power and originality' of the Direct Method teaching, and believed it 'should have a most useful influence on the general methods of classical work throughout the country.'[131] A second inspection, in 1910, reported that the 'brilliant work in classical and modern languages' was well known. 'Some difficulties', however, were 'due to inaccurate filling in of forms sent by the Board; this is rather characteristic of the school'. This was, in part, the entirely predictable result of Rouse's continuing concentration on teaching: he had no office, and spent his time in his classroom. But it also stemmed from his related dislike of forms, clerks and bureaucrats. The HMIs' remarks will have been prompted by the difficulty the Board had in securing accurate information from Rouse, not only on pupils and curriculum, but in particular on the Direct Method teaching reported in the Board's pamphlet *The Teaching of Latin at the Perse School*, which had recently been published.[132]

The report of the full inspection of 1922 shows this blend of admiration and alarm in a developed form. 'Numbers proceeding to University continue to be unusually large'; but 'The school does not take the School Certificate examination, the head holding that to do so would interfere seriously with the methods of teaching. On the classical side this matters little, on the other the results are serious.' With diplomatic caution, the inspectors added that they 'feel the need to put this opinion on record, but do not want to put pressure on the Head Master to act contrary to his considered opinion...the Head Master is responsible for the school, not the inspectors.' Where, one wonders, did this leave the school governors? Looking, presumably, for support from the Inspectorate in their dealings with Rouse. When they met the HMIs, they asked for an opinion of him; the Chief Inspector replied that 'he was not an easy man to sum up. That he had an awkward side could not be denied. He was a first-rate teacher but not interested in administration. The essential fact was that he was a very fine man, who had devoted his life's work to the school.' Rouse was then invited into the meeting, and the governors raised matters of concern, presumably in the hope of gaining inspectorial support for their views. A major concern related to the School House: was it in order for him to run this as a private enterprise? The Chief Inspector replied that the governors should have control of the building; they responded that they had none at all. The office copy of the report carries an additional set of comments 'not for inclusion in the issued report'. 'The chairman of governors has died or retired; he seemed to let the Head Master go his own way. The new chairman is Bowes of the publishing firm, and is much more active. The result is that the governors are getting a much better grip of the affairs of the school, not perhaps without some friction with the Head Master, who is notoriously rather a difficult person.'[133]

Rouse retained control of his boarding house until he retired, but was persuaded to relinquish other areas of his kingdom; notably, the prep and pre-prep schools, which had been run as a private enterprise. Together with the evidence already given on his financial support for salaries, this reminds us that the Perse was very much Rouse's school. He thus stands at the end of a long line of Victorian headmasters – 'towers of men' – who carved out kingdoms on earth which realised, more or less successfully, their visions of the ideal. The most illuminating comparison is perhaps with Thring, Headmaster of Uppingham. Like Rouse, he began with an uphill struggle, used his own money, faced hostile governors and built 'the almighty wall' of chapel and classroom. Like Rouse, Thring transformed his faith into a sense of educational mission; he, also, was a 'radical conservative', totally committed to classical education, but determined to revivify it, especially for 'the average boy'. Furthermore, he, too, lived to see his personal creation decay into something more conventional.[134]

The writing was on the wall in Rouse's last few years at the Perse. The celebration of his retirement, as one might expect, concentrated on the glorious past rather than looking to an uncertain future. The Perse Players put on a Latin play written for the occasion, and a dinner was held in his honour in the school hall. Sir Fabian Ware, who presided, suggested that 'Dr Rouse had succeeded where others had failed for one reason above all others – his sturdy independence. Most Englishmen acknowledged three supreme authorities, their country, their king, and their God...and would have no mediator between themselves and each of the three. That was Dr Rouse...'.[135]

In the wilderness: the ARLT in the 1920s

The 'praising with faint damns' which the Direct Method had received from the Prime Minister's Committee came as a blow to the ARLT, but not an entirely unexpected one. The Council of the CA, which was heavily represented on the Committee, was regarded by Rouse's followers as rarefied in view and over-ready to compromise in action; the rift between the two bodies was not finally healed until the 1940s. Rouse's Association, nevertheless, had grounds for optimism. Its membership had more than doubled in 1920-1, and continued to grow steadily, reaching 400 in the mid-1930s. The embarrassing fact, in a male-dominated world, was that the new members were mostly women. In 1924, two-thirds of the 300 members were female; in 1930, the summer school was attended by four men and 40 women. At the committee meeting held during the school, it was agreed that it was important to persuade a man to direct the next school. The situation was complicated by the fact that the Association's only surviving member in university teaching, Dr Avery Woodward of Royal Holloway College, London, was a woman. In the circumstances, the committee decided not to ask her to direct the next summer school.[136] The Association's dilemma might, with hindsight, have been predicted. The independent women who formed a large part of the teaching force outside the public schools were receptive to doctrines which combined a sense of educational mission with practical prescriptions for teaching; and these were exactly what was offered by the Direct Method. The summer schools provided insulated settings in which conversion to the mission could take place. Participants were encouraged to use Latin and Greek as much as possible, and conversation classes, plays and debates were held in which English was banned. The switch from English to Latin and Greek had something of the same function as the discarding of ordinary clothes and donning of uniform characteristic of other 'total institutions': it symbolised and reinforced the remaking of selves. One result was that the schools attracted a sprinkling of distinctly eccentric individuals; a pupil of Rouse's reports that 'some of the women were pretty rum, and not even in teaching.'[137]

That the Association was becoming self-consciously aware of its nature and image is suggested not only by these alarms about the sex ratio of its membership, but also by several abortive attempts to change its name. The existing title was cumbrous, and in the opinion of some, 'gives a certain suggestion both of aggressive defiance and of conscious superiority, which causes uneasiness to many members.'[138] The committee agreed to suggest 'Association for Latin Teaching' and 'Association of Latin Teachers' as alternatives; a minority preferred 'Association for Research into Latin Teaching', which had the obvious advantage of retaining the original acronym. But whereas in the previous year, a large majority had supported the change to 'Association of Latin Teachers', opinion was now so divided that the matter was dropped. Rouse steered clear of the debate, contenting himself with a letter to the Secretary asking her to give the next meeting this message from him: 'Whatever the exoteric name of the Association may be, it should have for its esoteric, Masonic, or secret name Association of Real Latin Teachers.'[139] A gentle reminder, perhaps, that the letter killeth, while the spirit giveth life.

When he retired from the Perse in 1928, Rouse left the School House and moved to Histon Manor, on the northern outskirts of Cambridge. Here he lived the life of a country squire (indeed, he held the lordship of two manors, though these were in Suffolk). His sister Alice continued to keep house for him until her death in 1939, helped by an ex-navy man and his wife. Surrounded by piles of books in his large library, he lived the life of the retired bachelor scholar, very much in the style portrayed in memoirs of Victorian dons.[140] Ex-pupils, sixth-formers and staff from the Perse came to tea on Sundays, sometimes to read Homer with him. The news they brought from the school was not good. As might have been predicted, the governors had appointed a successor who could be counted on to remove those aspects of Rouse's kingdom to which they had taken most exception. School Certificate examinations were introduced; Science was emphasised; and Classics began to be undermined. The new Headmaster, H.A. Wootton, was also temperamentally opposed to the atmosphere of informality and delegation Rouse had built up. A man described even in the official school history as 'incredibly rude',[141] he liked to keep decisions in his own hands, and to communicate with his subordinates by means of typewritten notes. Rouse was apprised of events in the school, but there was nothing he could do. His pupil Arthur Peck, a Classics don at Christ's College, was now on the governing body, but made little headway when he tried to raise the Rousean standard there.

Carrying on the good fight (1928-50)

Rouse's was a long and, especially in the first decade, productive retirement. He continued to attend ARLT summer schools, and to publish articles on the virtues of the Direct Method in the few journals, like the New Education Fellowship's *New Era*, which were still interested enough to carry them. He also took composition classes for Girton College, which was not far away, and prepared the occasional pupil in Sanskrit for the Indian Civil Service examinations. A more novel venture was the recording of gramophone records of lessons and readings in Latin and Greek. This came about as a result of an approach from the Linguaphone Institute ca. 1930; the records appeared in 1932. The publicity leaflet for the *Linguaphone Latin Course* declares that 'LATIN COMES TO LIFE.... Here at last is the opportunity for everyone interested in new and better methods of teaching Latin to find out exactly what these new methods are, and how they work. The...Course enables you to *listen* to Dr W.D. [sic] Rouse, famous as one of the most original and progressive minds in modern education, actually taking a class of schoolboys through the first ten lessons of Latin, taught by the Direct method.'

The Latin Course consisted of five 10" 78 r.p.m. records housed in an album. The accompanying text book contains the text of the lessons, with introductory notes and suggestions. The texts, particularly those of the early lessons, include stage directions to remind the listener that in the classroom, movement and gesture form part of the process of explanation. Rouse's Preface makes his familiar claims for the Direct Method, but also makes clear his larger ambitions for the reform:

> This life and naturalness give a new spirit to the class...: those who are thus taught will not write depressing letters to the *Times*, describing how they have wasted their schooldays.... This method is in fact the remedy for the disease, which all feel in English education, but not all own to themselves.... I recommend it therefore confidently to the attention of all those who are anxious about our national destiny, as a help in the right direction.[142]

Fig. 4 The alliance of mind and machine. Rouse's hatred of machinery had extended to radio until he heard some of his favourite music on a set. Gramophones, however, he had used since 1902, when Lady (Lilly) Frazer gave one to the Perse School. His 78 r.p.m. Linguaphone recordings were made ca. 1930. [Perse School Archives]

Rouse dedicated the Latin Course to 'the intelligent chorus from the Perse School: Beacock, Stockbridge, Whitehouse' – three pupils whom he had borrowed to play the pupils' parts in the recordings. His other Linguaphone records were solo efforts. A Greek Course was not produced; even a company which offered courses in Esperanto, American English and Icelandic presumably felt that adequate sales were unlikely. But they did commission two records: a 10" of the sounds and alphabet of ancient Greek, and a 12" on which Rouse read passages from Demosthenes, Homer, Pindar and Sophocles. In the accompanying leaflet, he emphasises that ancient Greek used a musical tonic accent, not a stress accent as in modern English. In some cases, indeed, the 'tune' in a line of poetry forms part of the meaning; for Rouse, the coaxing element in Odysseus' offer of wine to the Cyclops in *Odyssey* IX is brought out by the use of the tonic accent. In the Direct method, these accents – the rise and fall of pitch – are learnt as the words themselves are learnt. 'And thus there is no need to drop Greek accents, as the Classical Association have lately recommended, in a counsel of despair. They are treating a symptom, and neglecting the disease; for the disease is a false method of teaching, and when a true method is substituted, the disease and symptom disappear together.'[143]

The emphasis on a musical tonic accent was not the only way in which Rouse explored the musicality of speech. As far back as 1897, he had corresponded about his ideas on Pindar with the classicist W.R. Paton, who had emigrated to Greece and lived on the island of Samos. Paton suggested that Rouse should try reading the text to music, and added, 'what music doesn't matter, unless it's a very violent polka'.[144] Rouse immediately set about finding the best musical accompaniment. He wrote to experts on Beethoven, asking which tunes might best suit Pindar's text, and also appears to have considered the Bach cantatas as a possibility.

Music was, in a way, as central to Rouse's approach to teaching as was drama. Both gave life to words: the first gave meaning to words via pitch, rhythm, dynamics, the second via movement. Together they gave life to the word by making it the expression of a whole person rather than a mute artefact. Rouse himself was both keen on singing and unafraid to sing in public. At dinners and other social occasions, he liked to sing Victorian songs, being especially fond of 'Villikins and his Dinah'; and one of his ex-pupils remembered that he would often appear in one of the lower forms' lessons and sing them a ditty he had just composed, 'with no accompaniment and with no loss of dignity'.[145] Just after the First World War, Basil Blackwell published his *Chanties in Greek and Latin, Written for Ancient Traditional Airs*. Some of the songs are versions of English favourites, such as 'John Peel'; some are developed from passages in classical literature; others again, as Rouse says in his Preface, 'came out of my own head'. Several are derived from the 'traditional songs which physic the pain of the labourer', and Rouse's intention is to physic the pain of learning: 'Children's songs and singing games...are easily learnt and easily remembered, and to sing them gives great pleasure.' At the same time, they incorporate useful vocabulary – Rouse points out that one of the Greek songs 'contains ten aorist participles...several...irregular verbs, and several idioms.' The tunes are nearly all traditional European melodies; the only one drawn from a published source is *My Boy Willie* (p. 30), which Rouse was understandably keen to include.[146]

This emphasis on singing, for Rouse a kind of serious fun, was central not only to his mission, but also to the resistance to it on the part of the public-school establishment. As the ex-pupil quoted above – by 1950, himself a Headmaster – said in his obituary of Rouse, 'How many members of the Headmasters' Conference would face such a routine with equanimity?'[147] The Direct Method was not conventionally dignified. It brought the master down from the dais – indeed some of the Perse boys took the master's part in some lessons, thus exposing both the intellectual and social aspects of his authority to risk. The social, because it made the teacher a participant in a conversation rather than a transmitter of knowledge to passive recipients. The intellectual, because that same conversation was always to a degree unpredictable. The sharp wits and extensive vocabulary which the Method aimed to produce in the pupil were *a fortiori* required of the teacher; and as many visitors to the Perse realised amid their admiration, few were equipped for the task.

Rouse's retirement gave him more time to help his friend Page in the editing of the Loeb Classical Library. The evidence is insufficient for a clear picture of any division of labour between them; in some cases, they seem to have commissioned translations on the basis of personal acquaintance. Under this heading, for example, comes the translation of Sidonius Apollinaris, which was allotted to Rouse's ally in the early days of the Direct Method, E.V. Arnold. Arnold left the translation unfinished on his death in 1926, and Rouse engaged W.B. Anderson of St John's College, Cambridge, to complete the job. The arrangement was complicated by the existence of Arnold's partial drafts, some revised by Rouse, some unrevised. Rouse sent Anderson not only Arnold's drafts, but also relevant texts and commentaries from his own library. This was in the spring of 1927. A year later, Rouse sent a pacifying letter to Anderson, who had clearly been asked for a progress report and resented it:

> Please do not be annoyed. I do not want to transfer the work, only to
> get it done at some not too distant time. You see, you do not answer
> letters.... Can you give me a rough idea when you will be able to
> print? *We* have to arrange a number of books in advance.

Anderson eventually agreed to supply a first volume at the end of the year,
and Rouse wrote to him in relief, 'All's well that ends well'. In fact the end
was still some way off. Not until 1935 was Rouse able to read Anderson's
introduction. Even then, he was clearly obliged to encourage the dilatory
translator: 'The book is so nearly ready, that the delay is difficult to understand...'.[148]

A much happier correspondence resulted from Rouse's involvement
with the Loeb edition of Nonnos's *Dionysiaca*. A young American classicist, Louis R. Lind, had written a thesis on the poem, and in 1937 wrote
offering to provide an edition for the Loeb Library. By a remarkable co-
incidence, Rouse was himself working on a Loeb translation at the time.
Notes on mythology were to be provided by H.J. Rose, and Rouse suggested that Lind should supply parallel notes on difficult passages in the
text. In his reply to Lind's letter, Rouse mentioned that his interest was
fifty years old: 'the late W. Robertson Smith sent me to Florence to collate
the ms. which I did in part – & then he died and my job was hung up.'[149]

Most of his efforts in the 1930s, however, went into translation. Some of
this was a matter of duty, like his translation of the *Dionysiaca*; which he
confessed to finding wearisome.[150] The bulk of his output, however, represents a further attempt to convey the freshness and immediacy of the living
word: this time, to those without Greek; for the authors he chose to trans-
late were all Greek. For Rouse, the Greeks had foreshadowed Christianity,
whereas the Romans had tried to crush it. He wrote to Ezra Pound in
December 1934 that he had translated Apuleius' *Golden Ass*, which he saw
as the classical equivalent of Bunyan's *Pilgrim's Progress*, and also a set
of Roman Stories; but these were not so good 'because the Romans were
cruel and coarse.'[151] This was a message to which Pound will have been
receptive, since he had long ago declared that 'since the study of Martial
there is nothing I approach with such nausea and disgust as Roman life'.[152]

It is not entirely clear why Rouse took this extreme line (which is not,
however, unknown among Hellenists). His views seem to have sharpened
after his retirement, though even in the Loeb promotional pamphlet he
wrote in 1911 it is clear that his enthusiasm for things Roman was less
strong than his adulation of all things Greek. His consistent view that the
forces of goodness were generally in a beleaguered minority may have

been reinforced by an identification with the early Christians; in which case, Rome would obviously have at best an ambiguous status.

Dr Rouse and Mr Pound

The letter to Ezra Pound quoted above was the second Rouse wrote in a correspondence which lasted for several years, and which led to the publication of his translation of the Odyssey in 1937.[153] It was, in many ways, a remarkable epistolary relationship. For more than thirty years, Rouse had preached the gospel of directness and spirtual renewal. After initial successes, he had been rebuffed by the humanist establishment of which he was an increasingly marginal member. The world had stopped listening to him, and he had withdrawn from it to Histon, just as he had, though with more vigorous hopes, withdrawn to the School House twenty years before. Now, in a matter of months, he found a listener who not only did not turn away when the message was repeated, but demanded more. Rouse had read Pound's *Spirit of Romance* some years before, and had been inspired by it to explore the poetry of the troubadours; in 1934, seeing Pound's name on a new book, he had picked it up and read it; it was *Make it New*, published not long before.[154] Within a year, we find Rouse responding to Pound as pupil to master; accepting, for instance, that a translation of Homer was impossible, and that paraphrase of some sort had to be attempted instead. Where Rouse had tried to persuade his audience to listen directly to the words of the Greeks, Pound insisted that he must go through the text to the patterned energies beneath it. For Rouse's doctrine of the 'living word', he substituted that of the 'life beneath the words'.

The two men, of course, had the experience of English literary culture in common. Pound had been at the centre of the Edwardian literary movements which Rouse had lived through. While Rouse was struggling to break through the crust of public-school classical routine, Pound was putting on poetic masks – the *Personae* – in order to free himself from a similarly encumbering Victorian technique and vocabulary. It did not follow that their literary tastes were at all similar. Rouse was resolutely antimodernist, and the most recent author he really enjoyed reading seems to have been Charles Dickens. He published two books of selections from the novels, and had often read passages to the boarders in the School House on Sunday evenings. Describing this in 1933 in a letter to another of his correspondents, he adds but I missed out in *Great Expectations* the latter part, lovemaking and so on, which is just tacked on.... I see a young woman has just written a book in which Scott, Dickens & co are 'best sellers', and the real thing is this diseased Lawrence clique, and that grotesque man who has made up words to suit his own muddled mind. I have forgotten his name. An Irishman, I think.[155]

In his correspondence with Pound, the question of Rouse's views of modern literature, perhaps luckily, rarely arose. At one point Rouse offered some dismissive opinions, but as it happened, they coincided with Pound's: 'As for the modernists, Sitwell and co, they are idiots, so far as I have managed to read, without either sound or sense...'.[156] What did Rouse make of Pound's poetry? The question only arises once. Pound had apparently asked for an opinion of two books of the Cantos; Rouse replied:

> ...about your epic. I have two vols. but I have not read them through yet; it needs a concentrated effort which I am not equal to just now, & I can only say that they seem to be materials for a work, but I want to see the work itself. It has no form yet, & without form it cannot charm.[157]

However different their tastes in literature were in some respects, for both men Greek symbolised a freshness and freedom which promised the release they sought from inert ideas and tired words. Rouse's encomium of all things Greek has already been quoted from his Loeb pamphlet of 1912. In the same year, Pound wrote of one of Hilda Doolittle's imagist poems, 'It's straight talk, straight as the Greek!'[158] It did not follow that the two would agree on the definition of 'straight talk'. Certainly some of Pound's language must have come as a shock to Rouse. 'Bitch' and 'bastard' came easily from Pound's pen, and he sometimes lurches from a discussion of poetic language to denunciatory rage: 'What is usually called 'poetic prose' is to me slush, never has impact ENOUGH. and damn the Bible, lock stock and barrel and to hell with jew mythology, Calvin, Milton and the wh/dn/ caboodle.'[159] Or again, in the following year, 'as Wilson's putridity comes to light NOW, in the same way the great and enormous fahrt that was England from 1930 to 1936 will stink in futurity.Which said, let us return to Olympus...'.[160]

Pound had left England after the war, disgusted at the 'drawing rooms' whose inhabitants, he claimed, cared nothing for literature. He had also drawn fire from what he characteristically called 'the professional bastards...full of hate for anyone not in the gang' who denounced his creative (mis)translations of Greek.[161] It must have been the final straw when he found that 'according to a recent, damn edition/ all my interest in Sapphics has been due to accent misprinted in an old edition/ I just d/n well DON'T believe it, If so it is the most fecund literary error that has been for 2 centuries.'[162] Rouse had also had his difficulties with professors. D.S. Robertson, the Regius Professor of Greek at Cambridge in the 1920s, returned an interpretation of Pindar sent him by Rouse, with a brief note saying that he had no time to look at it. By the time he retired in 1928, most of the classical scholars of his own generation had gone; Postgate, Ridgeway and Arnold, for example, had all died in 1926. Both Rouse and Pound, then, were living in 1934 in a kind of self-imposed exile: Rouse in retirement at Histon, at the edge of Cambridge, his cause 'praised with faint damns' and the world he had created at the Perse severely damaged by his successor; Pound at Rapallo on the north-west coast of Italy, at the edge of the man-made world and next to the sea Homer had described. 'When they built the concrete sea-wall here, they bitched the sonority of the water/ it stayed bad for over a year and then, little by little, Poseidon took back part of his own proper noise', he reported gleefully to Rouse in 1935.[163]

One of the things about Rouse which endeared him to Pound was that he had sailed the Aegean in the wake of Odysseus, collecting folk tales. Hence his appearance in Canto 74:

and Rouse found they spoke of Elias
in telling the tales of Odysseus...

Pound is probably referring to the story Rouse heard on one of his Aegean voyages, perhaps in 1905, when the skipper in whose caïque he was travelling told how the prophet Elias (i.e., Elijah), who was a fisherman, became tired of the sea. He walked inland with an oar, asking each stranger he encountered what it was he was carrying, until he met someone who failed to recognise it, and described it as a stick. At that point, ' "Good!" said St Elias, "this is the place for me, here I abide." He plants his oar in the ground, and that is why his chapels are all built on the hill tops.'[164]

A debt of another kind, which sustained Pound through his occasional rages against Rouse's drafts of his Homer translations, derived from the publication of Arthur Golding's translation of Ovid, which Rouse had edited for the Temple Classics in 1905. When he first received one of Rouse's translations, Pound wrote

Before opening yr/ Ulysses I want to say how glad I am to know you are still in the land of the living, and to extend both hands of fellowship to the editor of Golding's Ovid.... By getting that into print, you have done more for my pleasure than perhaps any man living.

Your aim is absolutely RIGHT.... Can I be of any use?[165]

That last query implies, almost, respectful subordination; a tone continued in Pound's next letter, which begins:

Thanks very much for permission to quote letter.

Re/new version, I think it is immensely worth while.

My wife read the Ulysses, and my father is in the midst of it, enjoying it hugely.[166]

Rouse's drafts were, in fact, read by several members of Pound's household, or as he calls it, 'my entourage'. For Pound, one of the touchstones was his father's reaction. This was not just because his name was Homer, but also because his youth had been spent in wild country among both settlers and Indians. His experience of the use of the bow, for example, was passed on by Pound to Rouse when they were discussing the bow-stringing scene at the end of the Odyssey.

For two years or more, the exchange of drafts and comments continued. At first, all went smoothly; Pound was 'DEElighted' with the first section he saw. Soon they were deep in details. Some of Rouse's proposals were an immediate hit, like the phrase 'them as comes a'courting she'. Others Pound thought too stilted, and missing their common goal of living directness: 'NO NO Doc. Here you are backslidin' on all your highly respekkabl principles, and slinging in licherary langwidg and puttin' your sentences all out of whack'.[167] The problem was caused by Rouse's using words like 'plight', which Pound claimed never to have heard used while he was in England. Rouse explained that he had learnt 'natural' English from his parents and their friends, and from talking to peasants; Pound similarly referred back to his father as an authority. 'Natural' language was thus the product of idiomatic experience; and while George Henry Rouse had always striven for plain, direct language in his translations, his son had absorbed a variety of English educated talk of the 1860s and 1870s. As for Pound, he implicitly acknowledged the status of his language as idiolect by referring to it as 'my Rocky Mountain Gothic'. To some extent, of course, the two men were separated by what Dylan Thomas later called 'the barrier of a common language'. Pound acknowledged this by referring to his language as 'murrkan':

alas, as you are writing english, you can't call THEM THERE
BLOODY gallants, cake-eaters or lizzards. dudes, gigolos, young
scum. I suppose my native tongue is still more flexible than English.
good for nothing young sprigs, fils a papa, spooners, saps.[168]

Pound proved a hard taskmaster. He insisted that a firm narrative drive
must be maintained; the reader must be able to move at some speed
through the story. But this did not mean that the work of translation could
be accomplished at speed:

> Dear Doc Rouse
> YOU are a SCANDAL. Even Gavin Douglas had the decency to
> spend several months on the Aeneid.
> WHADDA you think this is a BEAN feast!![169]

And later the same month,

> I simply don't believe that any man could do the MASTERWORD
> that a definitive english Odyssey should be, at the speed you are
> going.
> who makes the living line must SWEAT, be gheez![170]

A more serious problem was that, as I have mentioned, whereas Rouse
saw the life of the story as contained in the text, for Pound the text was a
manifestation of a pattern of energies existing at a deeper level. It is this
doctrine which underlies comments like 'When I suggested a translation
with ALL the meaning, I didn't mean merely put back WORDS, or translations for words'.[171] Or this: '...I'd like to see a 'rewrite' as if you didn't
know the WORDS of the original...'.[172] Despite this doctrine, however,
Pound sent several letters which focus in detail on nuances of style, tone
and rhythm.

When his *Ulysses* was finished, Rouse went on to the Iliad, and the
process began again. A torrent of advice and complaint arrived from
Pound, interspersed with storms of rage directed at other Englishmen.

> Before reading yr/ letter and before answering or having further
> dealings with ANY Englishman whatever I wish to say that a nation
> which lets a flat chested shit of a codfish's cunt like Chamberlain
> steal 85% of my advance royalties on Cantos 41/51 is not a nation of
> men but of lice...
> ever cordially yours.

Can you tell me ANY way to get a message past Chamberpots buggering secretaries so that the chief poop wd/ have to see it?[173]

When he encountered Pound, Rouse had spent over thirty years preaching the gospel of vigorous, direct speech to an audience which appeared not to be interested. As the last quotation indicates, what he received from Pound was his own message, amplified and distorted by the megaphone of Pound's own obsessions. Both men had a constant message, and survived by finding new audiences for it. But in Rouse's case, this particular audience must have given him a considerable shock, as it moved from enthusiastic support to constructive but often violent criticism.

Pound's approval of Rouse stemmed in part from the latter's work for the Loeb Library. Pound had, indeed, once proposed to write a book based on a survey of the Library. A literary agent with whom Pound was in touch wrote to Rouse in 1937:

Ezra speaks of a project he once mentioned to you: a book length 'review' of the Loeb Library, 'excerpts to be ample and include whatever Greek and Latin (in translation) a sane non-specialist man might *now* take an interest in – a new assessment of Greek and Latin classics *now* confronted with world culture'.

And he adds...that the book would have to be done with consent of the publishers of Loeb and probably be published by them. What is your candid opinion of this, and if it is favourable would I or you best start the ball rolling?[174]

Nothing more is heard of this intriguing project; but by this time, Rouse must have become aware how difficult it would be to carry on with Pound the kind of discussion it would have necessitated.

The letters from Pound stopped in 1940. By then, Rouse had a less difficult correspondence in progress with Lind, by this time Professor of Classics at the University of Kansas. The Loeb edition of Nonnos had been published in 1939, but Rouse and Lind carried on writing to one another until 1947. Books and photographs were exchanged, and Rouse experimented with translations from Spanish, which was Lind's wife's first language. During the war, life at the Manor became difficult. Alice had died in 1939; both Rouse and the couple who kept house for him were getting too old to cope with the large garden and with repairs to the house. (His cousin, Clive Rouse, remembers snow falling through holes in the roof, which had to be shovelled out of the attics.) Food was scarce, the sky a source of imminent peril from bombs. What kept Rouse's spirits up were his books and his epistolary friends. His relationship with Lind could certainly be described in these terms. At one point, Lind offered him hospitality if he was willing to go to the USA. Rouse declined, but with a gratitude which warms the page of his letter. At the same time, he was conscious that he could not have long to live: one of his last letters to Lind reports that 'I am now 84, and must surely die soon.'[175]

The work which engaged him most in his last years was a translation of Pindar into both prose and verse, with an introduction which emphasised the subtle interconnexions and cross-references within the poems. Lind, at least, appeared to approve: 'The intricate cross-echoes have never been so thoroughly analyzed.... Your work lets all the wind out of Gildersleeve's objections to Metzger's analysis of the recurrent word...'.[176] Constructive criticism of the translations came from another correspondent, George Sampson, who first wrote to Rouse in 1940. Sampson was a man after Rouse's own heart. Born at Greenwich, with seafaring connexions – always a good point for Rouse, who saw the seadogs of the Elizabethan era as soulmates – he had been influential in promoting the serious study of English in schools, and had written the *Concise Cambridge History of English Literature*. Despite all this support, however, Rouse's Pindar was never published. He sent the whole manuscript to Lind in 1940, partly for safe keeping, partly because Lind had some hopes of finding an American publisher. His attempts failed, and the manuscript was sent back to England in 1947.

Although his Pindar was the work Rouse most wanted to see in print, he also translated all of Sophocles' plays, most of Aeschylus and some Euripides. In 1948 he sent these to the novelist Dorothy Sayers, with whom he had been corresponding, and asked her to show them to E.V. Rieu, editor of the Penguin Classics, then a very new series. At the end of the year she sent him a tactful and illuminating reply:

I did approach Mr Rieu, but...his own manner of translating the Classics is highly idiosyncratic, and very different from your own....
I can't find any other publisher who is interested in Translated Classics at the moment – very likely because the Penguins are rather occupying the field, and they are waiting to see what happens to them.
I think too, perhaps, that although your translations are very pleasant to read and contain many lines of quite remarkable beauty, they are not quite in line with the present fashion in these things, which inclines to a rather disconcerting exploitation of modern speech-idiom and what one might call post-Hopkins sprung rhythm.

She went on to add some detailed comments which are reminiscent of some of Pound's complaints about Rouse's drafts for his Odyssey:

> I have noted down one or two...expressions with which any actor would have difficulty.... In the *Prometheus*, for example: expressions like 'cowhorned maid', 'terrificationings' and the old-fashioned 'gore' for blood are apt to strike the actor as comic, and embarrass him; and the phrases 'kick back the bed of Zeus'...and 'intolerable you would be if healthy' are so remote from common spech that he would never be able to speak them with any conviction. Similarly in the *Agamemnon*:...'no more than dyeing bronze' (this would inevitable sound like 'dying' and be unintelligible to the audience); and above all, 'He falls – watery pan receives the load'. There is only one 'pan' which that will suggest to anybody (to be sure it is to be found in many bathrooms!!) and no actor could possibly say the line and get away with it.[177]

Amid such disappointments, Rouse was cheered by the successful careers of two of his ex-pupils, Frank Lockwood and Cyril Peckett. Both became headmasters, and both carried on and adapted the Direct Method for the next generation. Lockwood was especially close to Rouse, who became godfather to his son. Eloquent, impulsive and impatient of organisational detail, reluctant to put down on paper the word whose life came from speech, he resembled his master in more ways than one. He was very successful as a headmaster, and narrowly missed appointment as Headmaster of the City of London School (T.B.L. Webster, then Professor of Greek in the University of London, who was a member of the recommending committee, wanted to put him at the top of the list, but found that an alphabetical order was mandatory).[178] Peckett's particular contribution was twofold. First, he confronted the recurring problem with Direct Method, that it demanded teachers with more knowledge and gifts than were common in the profession, by producing textbooks which translated the method into pragmatically teachable terms.[179] Second, he set up a humanities course which acted as a support for the Classics teaching in his school. This had the incidental advantage of attracting favour from HMIs, who were in general still suspicious of the 'cult' aspect of the Direct Method and the ARLT.[180] Lockwood and Peckett were also instrumental in building bridges with the CA. After the Second World War, they took part in two initiatives in this area. Reading competitions were encouraged in the local branches of the CA to promote interest in spoken Latin and Greek.

Since literary texts were chosen for the competitions, the CA's emphasis on high culture and that of the ARLT in spoken language were neatly linked. In addition, a series of weekend courses was launched as a joint venture between the ARLT and the London branch of the CA. This too was a constructive compromise: the spirit of the summer school, compressed, adapted and brought within the reach of the average Classics teacher.[181]

In 1948, it became clear that the old man could no longer cope by himself, and he moved to Hayling Island in Hampshire to live with two female cousins. Most of his large library had to go, and Rouse issued a summons to several of his ex-pupils. Arthur Peck, as a Fellow of Rouse's old college, was instructed to select the most valuable books for transfer to the library at Christ's College: they are now housed together there, resplendent in leather bindings. In the obituary he wrote for the Perse School magazine *The Pelican*, Peck remembered how Rouse had made this potentially depressing event into a cheerful occasion:

> Just before he left Histon Manor I was there with him helping to divide up his books.... There was no wholesale throwing out, no haste to be through with a distasteful business, but each book was looked at and commented upon, almost as a living thing, and his cheerfulness and at times almost hilarity during this painful parting was something that can never be forgotten.[182]

Several other ex-pupils, all well established in schools, also received the call, and came in cars and vans to carry away their allotted share. In his new home in Hayling Island, Rouse carried on working: to this period can be assigned a virtuoso Greek version of the Lord Chancellor's patter-song from Gilbert and Sullivan's *Iolanthe*, done into the original metre. At the beginning of 1950 he fell ill, and died on the 10th February. He was buried at Histon a few days later.

Afterword

I suggested at the beginning of this memoir that Rouse was of particular interest because he was both central and marginal to the Edwardian defence of classical education. The course of his life reflects this combination of centrality and marginality, moving as it did from Calcutta, via 'little England beyond Wales', to London, and finally to Cambridge: a city in the country, in touch with the metropolis, yet too far away to become a suburb. In Cherry Hinton, and later at Histon, Rouse lived on the margin of the urban world. But this margin was, to him, the separate world which he created. There were other mid-Victorians who, like him, watched the decay of moral England as the railways spread over the countryside, what Kenneth Grahame's biographer has called 'The tyrannous emptiness of a society which was rapidly losing its spontaneity'.[183] Grahame, who was a contemporary of Rouse's, went through the conventional classical grind which Rouse denounced, and himself denounced it in much the same terms, describing the 'ignorance tempered by insubordination' with which he 'wrestled with the inflections of some idiotic language long rightly dead'. Grahame eventually found a use for the classics, if only as 'an adjunct to his own myth'.[184] The Great God Pan presides, however distantly, over the riverine world of *The Wind in the Willows*.

A concentration on childhood, on an innocence which is lost with the advance of material civilisation, was a common theme in the writing of those who felt as Rouse and Grahame did. Grahame lived a double life, working in the Bank of England by day, on his myth in the evenings. Similarly Charles Dodgson, the conservative Oxford don, switched from mathematics and symbolic logic to tea with the young and immersion in the world of Alice. And we might add Housman to the list, forced into a metropolitan exile by his failure at Oxford, following an ascetic ideal of scholarship, while lamenting (as Pound maliciously summarised it in his *Polite Essays*), 'Woe is me, London is bad, Shropshire is good'. All three compartmentalised their lives; Dodgson the most rigidly.[185] Rouse did not, precisely because his profession was one in which he could realise his vision. The world he built up at the Perse was a kingdom on earth, insulated from the outside, in which freshness, directness and innocence could, for a while, be restored.

The setting up of the prep and pre-prep schools guarded the Perse against the outside world at the point of entry. On leaving the Perse, however, some pupils faced a problem of adjustment to a world which was not run on Persean lines. Even his best pupils, who were well equipped in conventional terms, having won scholarships and read widely in Latin and Greek, sometimes encountered difficulties when they engaged with the conventional demands of the ordinary world. Peckett, who won a scholarship to King's College in the 1920s, found that he had already read most of the passages which confronted him in his examinations there. On the other hand, his reading of Greek, in the reformed pronunciation and complete with tonic accent, marked him out among his contemporaries, and when Greek plays were read, he was given the choral odes. What was technically the most accurate representation of the sounds of ancient Greek was in conventional terms deviant, both in the pronunciation of the vowels and in its being, in effect, sung.

The obsessive and missionary nature of Rouse's activities was bound to rouse the hackles of the conventionally minded. The great culture hero of classical scholarship in Rouse's first years at the Perse, Sir Richard Jebb, Regius Professor of Greek at Cambridge, consistently emphasised the serene and balanced aspects of ancient Greece; himself the author of a massive edition of Sophocles, he could hardly bear even to discuss Euripides, the sceptical questioner who dealt with the unserene and the irrational.[186] An alternative tradition, never so securely institutionalised, subversive of the Sophoclean serenity of Jebb, can also be traced: a tradition whose presiding deities were Pan and Dionysus rather than Apollo. This tradition can be seen in the reading of Nonnos's *Dionysiaca* which formed part of Percy Shelley's and T.L. Peacocks's rebellion against the conservative mood of the 1810s;[187] and in Oscar Wilde's citation of Theocritus' second Idyll, the *Pharmaceutriae*, as a work characteristically ignored in Jebb's articles on Greek literature in the *Encyclopedia Britannica*.[188] It is this tradition, perhaps, which forms part of the background to Rouse's abortive attempt to collate MSS of Nonnos during his fellowship at Christ's; though Rouse's own ruralism was deeply conservative. The figure of Cheiron, the wise centaur, half man, half beast, may stand as a symbol of the learning which fed on this tradition, a scholarship which delighted in the enthusiasm and irrationalism so deplored by Jebb, and which sought to (re)unite rational investigation with natural instinct. This is surely why Cheiron was an important figure in Grahame's myth;[189] why

'Cheiron' was Jane Harrison's pet name for Murray.[190] And this tradition perhaps gives added resonance to what might otherwise seem an insignificant pleasantry: Rouse's friend Fowler addressed him as 'Centaur', because he was full of wisdom and arrived at Fowler's house on horseback.[191]

From the 1900s through to the 1950s, what evidence there is for the private opinions of HMIs suggests that some of them, at least, saw the Direct Method movement as a cult whose enthusiasm might lead it beyond the bounds if not of sanity, then surely of convention. Certainly the plunge into the use of Direct Method entailed the taking of risks. Risk-taking was, for Rouse, an inevitable part of his radical solution to the nation's problems. But against the background of the moral panics of the 1900s – the fear of the 'mob', of the power to be exerted by 'our future masters' – the majority preference was for a curriculum which emphasised discipline rather than creativity, the rigid boundaries of Latin grammar rather than the risky fluidity of speech.[192] It was the dominance of this view after the war which led to the fossilisation of the four-year Ordinary level Latin course in English secondary schools. By the late 1930s, it was generally admitted that this was a failure.[193] Few of those who began it, reached the end. Those who did, had been drilled in grammar and learnt set books by heart. But the reality of the life of the ancients hardly entered their experience. As one HMI summed it up in the early 1930s, the course was characterised by 'thoroughness and unreality'.[194]

Yet the spirit of Rouse's mission survived. The work of his epigoni after the Second World War, broadening the Method, making it more accessible to the average teacher, co-operating with the CA in setting up new institutional forms, brought the spirit of directness into contact with the ordinary world of Classics teaching. The new Latin courses of the 1960s, conceived in the aftermath of the collapse of Compulsory Latin at the end of the previous decade, reacted against the dead hand of the paradigm in what may seem a different direction. Both the *Cambridge Latin Course* and its Scottish equivalent, *Ecce Romani*, set Latin narratives in Roman contexts, substituting for the everyday alienness of Latin grammar the alienness of everyday life in the ancient world. But they seek to immerse the pupil in a lived experience, to give back to the printed word the meaning which came from sequential, oral utterence and social context. Latin as meaningful sound is emphasised by the use of taped readings – the modern equivalent of Rouse's Linguaphone records of thirty years earlier. The long process in which Classics has become decentred in English high culture, detached from its long-standing class associations, is now well under way. In consequence, it is perhaps now easier to take it seriously, for itself: as a basis for comparison with the present, rather than as material to be moulded by modern stereotypes. As Murray urged in the 1900s in his attack on *paracharaxis* [literally, forging currency], we should look at Greece, not Greek; at classical literature and philosophy, not at the connotations of class and status they carried in the late nineteenth century. In the short term Rouse's mission was perhaps bound to fail, given the absolutist demands of his utopianism, the reluctance of the public schools to experiment, and the daunting pedagogic and scholarly equipment which seemed to many observers to be demanded by the Direct Method. Here the very brilliance of Rouse's own teaching was to some as disheartening as it was stimulating. In the long term, however, the pressure he generated for emancipation from the 'grammar grind' of the late nineteenth-century public school contributed, in however subterranean a fashion, to the reforming movements and new courses of the 1960s. One of their fundamental features was an emphasis on the sound of a spoken language, to be listened to as a stream of meaningful sound, rather than pored over as a row of words on a page, a puzzle which was somehow not expected to make ordinary sense. The maintenance of this emphasis through the years of 'thoroughness and unreality' we owe in great part to Rouse and his gospel of the living word.

THE DAILY MIRROR, SEPTEMBER 5, 1949

"Alister Stewart, 12, of the Perse School, takes his turn at addressing the class. He's teaching them the Latin for "egg."

THE BOYS WENT BACK TO SCHOOL—FOR A ROMAN HOLIDAY

JOHN SMITH, 13, adjusted the black gown around his shoulders, set his mortar-board on his head a fraction more rakishly and turned from the blackboard.

Chalk in hand, he addressed the class easily—in fluent Latin.

John's "ordeal" was no schoolboy nightmare. He had chosen deliberately to spend a week of his summer holidays as a Latin guinea pig.

So had ten of his friends. The eleven boys left Shrewsbury on an expenses-paid holiday at Cambridge to demonstrate a "live Latin" course to teachers. They take turns with the mortar-board and gown. So do another group of boys from the Perse School, Cambridge.

As John spoke to his schoolfellows, scores of headmasters and masters sat in silent rows, watching, listening, making a note or two.

The boys spend an hour each day demonstrating a new method of teaching Latin.

Eighty-one headmasters and masters from all over Britain are attending the course, which is run by the Association for the Reform of Latin Teaching, at Leys School, Cambridge.

They watch a class of eleven-year-olds learning Latin for the first time, and another class, who already know the language, show how the method develops over five years.

And off duty John and his friends still talk the language of Ancient Rome—in the bath, at tea-time or in a rowing boat on the river.

For Latin isn't just a list of phrases in a grammar book to them—it's a language in which they can really say things.

Headmaster Cyril Peckett, 37, who brought the boys to Cambridge from the Priory County School, Shrewsbury, said: "They are all volunteers.

"Why learn Latin at all? One of the masters at the course said: 'I learned Latin and hated it. My son learns it this way and loves it.

"Latin teaches you to express yourself in the briefest and clearest way. In earlier times only the rich and leisured knew it."

RUDY SAV...

Fig. 5 A rare piece of tabloid publicity for Direct Method Classics: a *Daily Mirror* story on the 1949 Summer School in Cambridge. [Rouse Papers]

Notes

[Rouse's papers are now held at Christ's College, Cambridge. The majority are recently acceded and so far unlisted. Earlier accessions are referred to by box number.]

1. Rouse's opinion on this matter was probably widely shared: 'With the 19th century began the era of learning about the classics, which finally drowned them in a bog of commentaries.' *Language teaching in the 19th century*, p. 5. TS, Rouse Papers, box 113[i], Christ's College, Cambridge.

2. Compare the point made by William Calder about Loeb's motives for starting the Library: 'In his Library Loeb found an occasion to unite two passions, [J.W.] White's classical humanism and [C.E.] Norton's democratic liberalism.' W.M. Calder III, 'Ulrich von Wilamowitz-Moellendorff to James Loeb: two unpublished letters', *Illinois Classical Studies* 2 (1977), 315-32.

3. Turner, F.M., *The Greek Heritage in Victorian Britain* (Yale University Press, 1981), 120-1; and the references there cited, to which can be added: Ackerman, R.A., 'Some letters of the Cambridge Ritualists', *Greek, Roman and Byzantine Studies* 13 (1972), 209-31. The standard treatment is now R.A. Ackerman, *The Myth and Ritual School: J.G. Frazer and its Cambridge Ritualities* (NY, Garland, 1991).

4. Brink, C.O., *English Classical Scholarship* (Cambridge: James Clarke, 1986), chh. 7-9.

5. George Sampson to Rouse (7 September 1941): 'I was at table with Page on that last Friday he was at the Reform Club. Frank Swinnerton was in full tide of humorous anecdotes, and Page was chuckling in his large way, and saying, "You are really a very amusing fellow." The old boy had really quite a good time; and then he went off and we never saw him again.' Rouse Papers. Cp. Swinnerton's memories of Page at the Reform in his *An Autobiography* (Hutchinson, 1937), esp. 294-9.

6. Rudd, Niall, *T E Page* (Bristol Classical Press, 1991), 28, 35.

7. Winstanley, D.A., *Later Victorian Cambridge* (Cambridge University Press, 1947), 221.

8. On the misreading of Locke at this period, see H. Aarsleff, 'Locke's reputation in 19th-century England', *The Monist* 55 (1971), 392-422; since reprinted in Aarsleff's *From Locke to Saussure* (Minnesota University Press, 1982). On the motives behind this misreading, see also H. Aarsleff, 'Joseph de Maistre and Victorian thought on the origin of language and civilisation', in (eds) T. Bynon and F.R. Palmer *Studies in the History of Western Linguistics* (Cambridge University Press, 1986), 96-108.

9. Merz, J.T., *A History of European Thought in the 19th Century* (Blackwood, 1904-12), vol. III, ch. 2.

10. For Paley, see his entry in the *Dictionary of National Biography*, and in the *Biographical Dictionary of English Catholics*; his career and scholarship are discussed by C. Collard in (ed.) H.D. Jocelyn, *Tria Lustra, Liverpool Classical Monthly* (1992).

11. The posthumously issued *Fragments of Two Essays in English Philology* (Macmillan, 1873), derives from papers he gave in 1830 to a short-lived body known as the Cambridge Etymological Society.

12. On Trench and Müller, see L. Dowling, *Language and Decadence in the Victorian Fin-de-siècle* (Princeton University Press, 1986), ch. 2.

13. It should be stressed that these remarks are speculative; but supporting evidence could be assembled. A key figure is Samuel Butler, Headmaster of Shrewsbury from 1798 to 1836, who laid great stress on verse composition, promotion by merit and monetary rewards for scholastic distinction. See C.A. Stray, 'England, Culture and the 19th Century', *Liverpool Classical Monthly* 13.6 (June 1988), 85-90; and for the literary and political background, M. Butler, *Romantics, Rebels and Reactionaries* (Oxford University Press, 1982), who says of the years around 1800,

> The intellectual life of the capital contracted noticeably. There was an unmistakeable gentlemanly consensus whereby the extremisms of the last half-century, in style as in politics, were driven from the scene...the Enlightenment appeal to universals was insistently rebuked by an emphatic traditionalism, a fussy insistence upon the rules of grammar and metre, and knowledge of the classics. [p. 115]

14. Quoted from the Preface to Butler's *Some Leisure Hours of a Long Life* (Cambridge: Bowes, 1914) by Graham, E., *The Harrow Life of Henry Montagu Butler* (Longmans, 1920), 368. For Butler's passion for detail and ingenuity, see ibid. pp. 371-2.

15. For Cambridge, see S. Rothblatt, *The Revolution of the Dons: Cambridge and Society in Victorian England* (Faber, 1968); for Oxford, see A. Engel, *From Clergyman to Don* (Oxford University Press, 1983). These are critically supplemented by A.G.L. Haig, 'The church, the universities and learning in later Victorian England', *Historical Journal* 29 (1986), 187-201, which emphasises the central role of declining rates of graduate ordination in the professionalisation of academe.

16. A good account of their activities is provided by M.A. Laird, *Missionaries and Education in Bengal 1793-1837* (Oxford University Press, 1972).

17. King's College had been founded in 1828 as a religious counterpart to the aggressively secular University of London, founded in 1826, which was renamed University College, London, in 1836.

18. A useful account of the College is given by D. Kopf, *British Orientalism and the Bengal Renaissance: the Dynamics of Indian Modernization 1773-1838* (California University Press, 1969).

19. G.H. Rouse box, Baptist Missionary Society Archives. Similar sentiments are quoted in his obituary in *The Missionary Herald*, vol. 91, 145-8. Much of this translation was done by dictating from the Greek text in English to a Hindustani speaker, who then gave a Hindustani version to a group of dialect-speakers. An amusing anecdote of the alleged failings of the method is given by Thomas Love Peacock in a letter to Shelley (4 December 1820): the injunction 'Judge not, lest ye be judged', for example, became in some of the versions 'Do not justice, lest justice should be done to you'. Peacock was working under James Mill at India House at the time. Peacock, T.L., *Works*, (ed.) H.F.B. Brett-Smith and C.E. Jones (London: Constable, 1924), vol. 8, pp. 218-9.

20. The SUN is preserved in the Rouse papers, together with two other youthful efforts, the 'Rushlight' and the 'Comet'. They appear to date from ca. 1873.

21. Rouse, W.D.H., 'Old School Days', *Christ's College Magazine* 37 (1898), 107-15.

22. The college afterwards moved to Oxford. See R.E. Cooper, *From Stepney to St Giles* (Carey Kingsgate Press, 1960); which also reports that the faith of the non-lay students of the 1870s was often shaky:

> Towards the close of the year, the Commitee had the pain of finding that some of the students had abandoned, more or less, their old faith.... In the end two Students resigned, and two more were informed that with their present views they could not remain in the College. [College Report (1871); quoted, ibid. p. 63]

23. R.S. Conway, later Professor of Latin at Manchester, was best known for his work on Latin and the Italic dialects. Peter Giles, who became Master of Emmanuel College, Cambridge, published several works on comparative philology.

24. For the controversial Orientalist William Robertson Smith, see J.S. Black and G.W. Chrystal, *The Life of William Robertson Smith* (Black, 1912). For Rouse's return to the study of Nonnos, see below, p. 48.

25. On Cook, see C. Seltman, 'Arthur Bernard Cook, 1868-1953', *Proceedings of the British Academy* 38 (1952), 295-302. On Frazer, the definitive treatment is R.A. Ackerman, *J.G. Frazer: His Life and Work* (Cambridge University Press, 1987). For Ridgeway, see R.S. Conway, 'Sir William Ridgeway, 1853-1926', *Proceedings of the British Academy* 12 (1926), 327-36.

26. Peile to Rouse (7 January 1894). Rouse Papers.

27. Viëtor's work is discussed, his career outlined, and his pamphlet translated in A.P.R. Howatt, *A History of English Language Teaching* (Oxford University Press, 1984); the translation is at pp. 340-63.

28. Beale to Rouse (February and March 1895). Rouse Papers.

29. The testimonial is in Cambridge University Library, Cam.b. 899.16.

30. 'Town House' was founded in 1888 to help instil a sense of corporate identity in the dayboys at Rugby. The house was given its own Tutor – the equivalent of a housemaster in a boarding house – in 1891, and separate premises, the 'Town Room' in 1901. Hope Simpson, J.B., *Rugby since Arnold* (Macmillan, 1967), 125.

31. Brogan, H., *The Life of Arthur Ransome* (Cape, 1984), esp. 21-4. Ransome began his life as a newspaper correspondent in Moscow, where he played chess with Lenin; later in life he returned to England, where he wrote the *Swallows and Amazons* children's books for which he is most widely remembered.

32. Cannan to Doble (13 December 1899). Oxford University Press Archives, C/2/1/2.

33. Rouse, W.D.H., *Demonstrations in Greek Iambic Verse* (Clarendon Press, 1899), vi-vii.

34. Walrond to Tait (31 October 1869). Lambeth Palace Library, Tait MSS, 314-5.

35. Page to Rouse (12 December 1901). Rouse Papers. Sir Richard Jebb was Regius Professor of Greek, H.M. Butler was Master of Trinity College, Cambridge.

36. Page to Rouse (15 November 1897). Rouse Papers.

37. Page to Rouse (18 June 1893). Rouse Papers. Page was referring to the Rev. J.E.C. Welldon, who was once greeted by Henry Bradshaw with the magnificent rebuke, 'Well, Welldon, you lied: and what is worse, you knew you lied.' Annan, N., *Leslie Stephen* (Weidenfield, 1984), 235.

38. Page to Rouse (11 March 1910). Rouse Papers.

39. Rouse's applications and testimonials for Aldenham, Tonbridge and Warwick are in Cambridge University Library: Cam.b.896.5, b.898.9, b.899.16. For St Paul's see the printed Minutes of the Governing Body (25 May 1905), 93-4. A letter from Sir John Gorst to Rouse suggests that the latter was considering an application for the headship of Shrewsbury in 1908, but there is no evidence that he proceeded with this. Gorst to Rouse (17 March 1908). Rouse Papers.

40. Millington to Rouse (4 December 1901). Rouse Papers. Millington had also advised Rouse on the problems of a lay headmaster: in 1893, he told him that he himself had only accepted appointment to Bromsgrove on the understanding that the Bishop would allow him, though not ordained, to preach in the school chapel. Millington to Rouse (12 June 1893), ibid.

41. Caldwell Cook's ideas are discussed in D. Beacock, *Play Way English for Today* (Nelson, 1943). See also S.J.D. Mitchell, *Perse: A History of the Perse School 1615-1976* (Cambridge: Oleander Press, 1976), ch. 11. This is the major published source for information on Rouse's headmastership.

42. A.I. Tillyard to Rouse (4 February 1906). Rouse Papers. The two men had a more personal connexion, in a way, since Tillyard's daughter Aethelrida married the Greek poet Michaelides, who used the pseudonym Ephtaliotis (he subsequently joined the British consular service and changed his name to Graham). Given Rouse's commitment to all things Greek, both ancient and modern, this will have formed the basis of a personal relationship which may well have been crucial in the faltering early years of Rouse's experiment with Direct Method.

43. On progressive schooling, see R. Skidelsky, *English Progressive Schools* (Pelican, 1969); R.J.W. Selleck, *English Primary Education and the Progressives, 1914-1939* (Routledge, 1972). For the 'efficiency movement', see G.R. Searle, *The Quest for National Efficiency. A Study in British Politics and Political Thought, 1899-1914* (Blackwell, 1971).

44. *The Perse School.* Printed Statement for the Governors (1927).

45. Printed sheet entitled *Conspectus of the Perse Series*, n.d.

46. Memoranda on methods of teaching by Dr Rouse and Miss Sanders, for use of the [Classical Association] Curricula Committee (January 27th 1906), 7 pp. In the author's possession.

47. See note 36.

48. Headmaster's report to Governors. Perse School Archives.

49. *The Perse School, Cambridge. Speech by Mr S.H. Butcher, MP...July 11th, 1906.* Printed pamphlet, 4 pp. Perse School Archives.

50. Morant to Rouse (31 July 1905). Rouse Papers.

51. Board of Education to Rouse (13 November 1907). Rouse Papers.

52. This is apparent in the internal Board of Education memoranda preserved in the papers of J.W. Headlam (later Sir James Headlam-Morley), at the time Staff Inspector for Secondary Education at the Board. These have recently been deposited at the Churchill Archive Centre, Churchill College, Cambridge.

53. *Special Reports on Educational Subjects: vol. 20. The teaching of Classics in secondary schools in Germany.* Cmnd 4997. This report was issued in January 1910, but Headlam's visit to Germany had taken place in 1906. An adequate explanation for the delay is provided by Headlam's characteristic dilatoriness, which also delayed publication of his report on the teaching of literary subjects in secondary schools. This was based on inspectorial visits made in 1901, but was not published until late in 1903. Cp. his superior J.W. Mackail's complaint earlier that year: 'What has become of Headlam's Report on Inspected Secondary Schools, which was to be put in hand as long ago as February last, but of which I have yet heard nothing further?' Mackail to W.N. Bruce (5 June 1903). Headlam-Morley papers, Churchill Archive Centre, Cambridge.

54. *The teaching of Latin at the Perse School, Cambridge. Educational Pamphlets, no. 20. Educational Experiments in Secondary Schools, no. i.* HMSO 1910.
The teaching of Greek at the Perse School, Cambridge. Educational Pamphlets, no. 28. Educational Experiments in Secondary Schools, no. iii. HMSO 1914.

55. A draft timetable, undated but pre-1911, shows that out of a total of 36 teaching periods per week, Rouse spent 18 with the sixth form (of which a few were shared with the fifth); 6 with the fifth form; and had 12 free periods. Classical periods took up half the sixth forms' timetable.

56. *The teaching of Latin at the Perse School*, HMSO 1910, p. 22.

57. *The teaching of Greek at the Perse School*, HMSO 1914, pp. 30- 1. After his retirement, Rouse tried to capture those 'gleanings of the harvest' in his *Scenes from Sixth-Form Life* (Oxford: Blackwell, 1935), which is discussed below.

58. Rouse, W.H.D., *Scenes from Sixth-Form Life* (Blackwell, 1935). Rouse's statement is quoted from p. 6; his assailant was one W.C. Summers (not, so far as is known, the expert on Silver Latin of that name).

59. 'To school with Rouse'. Incomplete MS notebook by P.J.Copping, n.d., 28 pp. Perse School Archives.

60. Ibid. pp. 5-6.

61. Similarly with the reading of texts, where 'All the Sixth Form...were lumped together...and the pace was that of the fastest.... I remember that when I first went into the sixth form I was confronted with the *Agamemnon* of Aeschylus – my first introduction to Greek poetry. The gentlemen in the Upper Sixth...romped happily through the complicated choruses, while I trailed behind.... Yet...something of the meaning and something of the majestic grandeur of the poetry seeped through and that first taste of the sixth form was a thrilling if somewhat frightening experience.' A.W. Eagling, quoted in Mitchell, *Perse*, 113. Other reminiscences of Rouse's teaching are quoted by Mitchell, 111ff.

62. Rouse, W.H.D., and Appleton, R.B., *Latin on the Direct Method* (University of London Press, 1925).

63. The book was published in 1867 by Macmillan and edited by F.W. Farrar; the Preface, which was unsigned, was composed by another contributor, J.M. Wilson.

64. The first detailed studies of the last two have recently appeared. For the Clarendon Commission, see C. Shrosbree, *Public Schools and Private Education* (Manchester University Press, 1988); for the Taunton Commission, see D.I. Allsobrook, *Schools for the Shires* (Manchester University Press, 1986).

65. A sarcastic and irreverent view is provided by the following: 'The theory is that each boy faithfully learns from 40 to 70 lines of Greek or Latin verse each day, and in that way acquires a valuable store of classical matter for the thought of after years. A certain portion is no doubt thus fixed rather strongly in the memory; and for proof we may refer to the fact that about nine-tenths of classical allusions made in the House of Commons are derived from the first book of the Aeneid.' 'Eton Quotations', *Academia* (22 January 1868), 93, quoting from the *British Quarterly Review*.

66. *Fortnightly Review* 72 (November 1902), 866-80. Postgate was at this time the senior Latin scholar at Cambridge. A man of great energy and an efficient organiser, he had previously acted as the first Secretary of the Cambridge Philological Society, and went on to fill a similar position in the Classical Association of England and Wales, founded in 1903 as a direct result of the publication of his article.

67. Cole, Margaret, *Growing up into Revolution* (Longmans, 1949), 5-7.

68. For an account of the tensions between Rouse, the association he founded in 1913, and the Classical Association, and for background on the defence of Classics in the 1900s, see C.A. Stray, 'Culture or discipline? the redefinition of classical education', in (ed.) M.H. Price, *The Development of the Secondary Curriculum* (Croom Helm, 1986), 10-48.

69. Headmasters' Conference *Bulletin* (1917), 62ff.

70. *Idem* (1902), 26-38.

71. W.G. Rushbrooke to Rouse (4 November 1903). Rouse Papers.

72. Crees, J.H.E., *Didascalus Patiens* (Smith Elder, 1915), 167-8.

73. Headmasters' Conference *Bulletin* (1907), 68.

74. Mitchell, S.J.D., *Perse*, 87. pp. 85-95 of this work contain a number of other details of Rouse's appearance and habits.

75. Draft testimonial from J.L. Paton (4 June 1901). Rouse Papers.

76. Bayles' comments raise the question of punishments. My impression that Rouse was not a flogger, but would cane pupils when he had to, is confirmed by John Mitchell, the Perse School historian, who adds, 'He believed strongly in corporal punishment, but mainly as a last resort; but when he wielded the cane himself he did not hurt the victim, but made him feel a worm.... The main punishment was a full afternoon's detention on a games afternoon; but a boy, with the permission of the master who gave the detention, could ask for it to be "swished off" by the Second Master.' (Letter to author, 4 September 1989.) Cp. P.J. Copping's memoir, referred to in note 59 earlier: 'Next morning I was haled to the Headmaster's study to be charged, lectured and punished – will two strokes of the cane, such easy, soft almost gentle blows...that I could scarcely believe it...'. [p. 27]

77. 'Classical work and method in the 20th century', *Scienza* 4 (1908), 3-36 at p. 4.

78. Benson, A.C., 'The place of Classics in secondary education', *The 19th Century and After* (November 1910), 868-76.

79. Rouse, W.D.H., 'The place of Classics in secondary education. A reply', *The 19th Century and After* (December 1910), 1082-6.

80. Rouse to the Governors (23 March 1913). Rouse Papers. For the 1927 statement, see note 36.

81. This inheritance may well have been considerable, as it came five years after a division of the family property in which George Henry was one of the principal beneficiaries.

82. Quoted from the extracts from Benson's diaries given by S.J.D. Mitchell, 'Arthur Benson and the Perse', *The Old Persean Chronicle* (January 1982), 16-19. Rouse is not to be seen in at least one photograph of the occasion: see D. Newsome, *On the Edge of Paradise. A.C. Benson: the Diarist* (London: Murray, 1980), opposite p. 274.

83. She is referred to in one letter as 'Kitty, that fair but frozen maid'; a reference to a riddle by David Garrick, quoted by Mr Woodhouse in Jane Austen's *Emma*. Some of Rouse's letters to Fowler are quoted in R.H. Coon, *William Warde Fowler* (Blackwell, 1934).

84. The texts edited by Rouse included Arthur Golding's translation of Ovid's *Metamorphoses* (1904). This was the publication which first drew him to the attention of Ezra Pound. Israel Gollancz was in charge of the *Temple Classics* (1896-) and the *King's Classics* (1902-). To the former series, Rouse contributed Milton's *Paradise Lost* (1897) and *Paradise Regained* (1898), Earle's *Microcosmographie* (1899), Bunyan's *Holy War* (1901) and Kinglake's *Eothen* (1901); to the latter, translations from Cicero (1900 and 1906) and Apuleius (1904).

85. *The public school spirit.* TS, Rouse Papers, box 113[i], Christ's College, Cambridge. Note the final phrase, which neatly encapsulates the Rousean equation of 'the real England' with the England of rural life.

86. Ellmann, R., *Golden Codgers* (Oxford University Press, 1977), 113-71, at pp. 116, 120, 121.

87. 'To young teachers', *Latin Teaching* 24.2 (June 1943), 25- 30.

88. *Journal of the Parents' National Educational Union* 48.6 (June 1937), 367-81, at pp. 370-1, 379, 381.

89. *The Perse School, Cambridge. An illustrated account of a pioneer public school. Its methods of education, games and institutions. With some opinions of public men.* Perse School Archives.

90. Professor Robert Skidelsky, the author of *English Progressive Schools* (Penguin, 1969), informs me that he has no memory of encountering any reference to Rouse during the research for his book.

91. Untitled MS in Rouse's hand, 10 pp., ca. 1912. Rouse Papers.

92. Ruskin to Rouse (29 May 1883). Rouse Papers.

93. Peckett, C.W.E., 'Caldwell Cook, Dr Rouse and the Perse', *Inspectors' Bulletin* (Department of Education and Science); new series no. 45 (July 1965), 11-16. I am grateful to Alan Turberfield HMI for making this article available to me.

94. Postgate, R.W., 'Portrait of a classical scholar', *The Listener* (11 September 1958), 373-4. Raymond, who was disinherited by his father because of his socialism and pacifism, was hardly an unbiassed witness. Yet his account is consonant with the views which emerge from his father's published utterances.

95. Skidelsky, R., 'Keynes and his parents', *Daedalus* 107 (1978), 71-9, at p. 76.

96. Housman, A.E., *The Confines of Criticism*, (ed.) J. Carter (Cambridge University Press, 1969), 34-5.

97. Nine volumes of diaries, recently found among the papers of Rouse's pupil A.L. Peck, are now in the library of Christ's College, Cambridge.

98. Cutting from unidentified journal, 1900s. Rouse Papers. A eulogy of the self-sufficient Greek peasant is contained in a lecture, later published, which Rouse gave to the Ruskin Society of Birmingham in February 1899 under the title *Peasant Life in Modern Greece.*

99. See Easterling, P.E., 'Greek MSS in Cambridge', *Transactions of the Cambridge Bibliographical Society* 4 (1964-8), 179-91.

100. Rouse to Professor (Oliver) Elton, n.d. but probably 1933. Rouse Papers.

101. See W.M. Calder III, 'Ulrich von Wilamowitz-Moellendorff to James Loeb: two unpublished letters', *Illinois Classical Studies* 2 (1977), 315-32.

102. Page to Rouse (7 January 1911). Rouse Papers.

103. *Machines or Mind?* (Heinemann, 1912), 5-6, 9, 11-12, 13.

104. *TES* (5 November 1912), 132a.

105. Lankester, E.R., 'Compulsory science vs compulsory classics', *The 19th Century and After* (March 1911), 449ff. Rouse, W.D.H., *The New Renaissance. An Answer to Ray Lankester* (Cambridge: Heffer, 1911), 13.

106. E.V. Arnold is best known for his *Roman Stoicism* (Oxford University Press, 1911), but was also an accomplished linguistic scholar who wrote on Greek, Latin and Vedic metre. He also published several introductory books on Latin.

107. Williams, J.G., *The University College of North Wales* (University of Wales Press, 1987).

108. *The Times* (11 September 1911).

109. *Report of the School of Latin Teaching* (1911). For the 'reformed pronunciation', see E.V. Arnold and R.S. Conway, *The Restored Pronunciation of Latin and Greek* (Cambridge University Press, 1895). The aim of the reformers was to promote a scheme of pronunciation which was at once close to ancient practice and standardised in English schools and universities. For the context of the reform, see C.A. Stray, op. cit. [n53].

110. The phrase 'to go the whole hog' means simply 'to do something thoroughly.' But 'whole hogger' and 'half hogger' were also in use at this time, specifically to describe degrees of assent to Joseph Chamberlain's proposals on Imperial Preference. It may therefore be significant that Frank Jones taught in Birmingham, Chamberlain's political stronghold.

111. For details, see Mitchell, *Perse*, 103-4.

112. In the terms used by the sociologist Max Weber, Rouse was thus an 'exemplary' rather than an 'ethical' prophet.

113. Crees, J.H.E., *Didascalus Patiens* (Smith Elder 1915), 168.

114. The basic source here is the Minute Book of the Classical Journals Board of the Classical Association, from which I quote by permission of its secretary, Professor C. Collard. The matter is also referred to in Godley's *Reliquiae*, (ed.) C.R.L. Fletcher (Oxford University Press, 1926). See vol. 1, pp. 322-9; vol. 2, p. 191.

115. *Latin Teaching* 1.1 (January 1914); editorial.

116. CA *Proceedings*, J. Murray (1914), 38-47; CA Council Minutes, CA Archives (7 February, 21 March, 6 May 1914).

ARLT Committee minutes (10 June, 28 February 1914), ARLT Archives.

117. The pamphlet was published by Heffer of Cambridge in 1909. Copy in Cambridge University Library, Cam.d.909.11. The fact that the Perse was in receipt of a special grant from the Board of Education is sufficient to explain Rouse's uncharacteristic (and to my knowledge unique) reluctance to put his name to what he published.

118. Rouse to Murray (22 November 1918). John Murray Archives.

119. Rouse, W.H.D., *Les Allemands peints par eux-memes* (London: Hachette, 1923). The book has a preface by Gaston David, the Jewish bookseller from whose stall in the Cambridge market square Rouse had been buying precious old volumes since the 1880s. Copy in Cambridge University Library, Ud.2.53.

120. Ironically, at one point Wells had considered sending his two sons to the Perse. He was put off the idea after reading an article written by Caldwell Cook. His letters to Rouse, preserved among the latter's papers, show that the two were united by their experience as assistant masters, and by their determination that education should be reformed, but by little else. It is difficult to believe that Wells would have sent his sons to a school which was, however progressive, still a classical school.

121. Education Guild (formerly the Teachers' Guild) *Report* for 1828-9 (Modern Records Centre, University of Warwick).

122. *Education Reform* (London: PS King, 1917), 78, 81.

123. Bodleian Library, MSS Gilbert Murray, boxes 419-27.

124. Ibid. box 420, f21.

125. Ibid. box 420, ff85ff., 104ff.

126. Ibid. box 420, f180.

127. *The Classics in Education*, HMSO 1921, pp. 144-7.

128. Lewis, L.W.P., *Practical Hints on the Teaching of Latin; being four lectures delivered...at the Board of Education's Latin courses in...1918 and 1919* (Macmillan, 1919), 3.

129. *Latin Teaching* 4.2 (June 1921); editorial.

130. Ibid. 4.3 (November 1921); editorial.

131. Public Record Office, Ed 109/269.

132. Ibid., Ed 109/270.

133. Ibid., Ed 109/271.

134. Thring has recently been the subject of a study by D. Leinster-Mackay, *The Educational World of Edward Thring* (Falmer Press, 1987).

This is intended to give a portrait of Thring, but ignores the grammars and other books he wrote as a result of a formative experience teaching children in an elementary school as curate in Gloucester in the 1840s. 'Radical conservative' is Thring's characterisation of himself: ibid., 27 note 74. The comparison cannot be pressed too far. Thring was a committed member of the established church, Rouse moved away from his Baptist faith. Corporal punishment was hardly a part of Rouse's system, whereas for Thring it was necessary, though used with care (see G.R. Parkin, *Edward Thring* [Macmillan, 1900], 266-73).

135. *Cambridge Chronicle and University Journal* (25 July 1928): 'Dr W.H.D. Rouse. Friends rise up and call him blessed. A niche in the hall of fame.' Cutting in the author's possession.

136. ARLT Committee minutes (1930).

137. C.W.E. Peckett, in conversation with the author.

138. ARLT Committee minutes (8 January 1924).

139. Rouse to Miss M.F. Moor (21 December 1923). ARLT Archives.

140. See, for example, R.W. Chapman, *Portrait of a Scholar* (Oxford University Press, 1917), on Ingram Bywater, Professor of Greek at Oxford.

141. Mitchell, *Perse*, 163.

142. *Linguaphone. The direct method applied to Latin.* Linguaphone Institute, n.d., p.6.

143. *Linguaphone. The sounds of ancient Greek and passages from the Greek classics.* Linguaphone Institute. n.d. (March 1932), 3. The point about Odysseus' speech is made on p. 4; the relevant passage (Homer *Odyssey* IX.347) can be heard on record. A refreshing note of realism (Rouse's opponents would have said, amateurism) is provided by his slips. Thus psi was 'inadvertently omitted' from the alphabet during recording of the 'Sound of Ancient Greek'; while in the Latin Course, Rouse gets his numerals in the wrong order: decem, duodecim, undecim.

144. Paton to Rouse (23 December 1897). Rouse Papers.

145. D.W. Hughes, obituary of Rouse, *The A.M.A.* (July 1950), 202.

146. All the quotations are from the (unpaginated) Preface to Rouse, W.H.D., *Chanties in Greek and Latin* (Oxford: Blackwell, 1922). 'My Boy Willie', which of course uses Rouse's own childhood name, comes from Cecil Sharp, *English Folk Songs*.

147. Ibid., p. 204.

148. Letters from Rouse to Anderson (1927-8, 1935). Rouse Papers, Christ's College, Cambridge. The first volume appeared in 1936; Volume II, after an even more protracted series of delays, in 1965.

149. Rouse to Lind (15 April 1937). From a typed transcript made by Lind and sent to the Perse School in 1978. 53 pp. plus introduction.

Notes

150. He had already produced Loebs of Lucretius (1924), and earlier of Seneca's *Apocolocyntosis* (1913).

151. Rouse to Pound (27 December 1934). Beinecke Library, Yale University.

152. Pound to Schelling (16 June 1907). Quoted in D.D. Paige (ed.), *The Letters of Ezra Pound, 1907-1941* (Faber, 1941), letter 1.

153. *The Story of Odysseus* (1937).

154. Rouse to Pound (4 January 1935). Beinecke Library, Yale University.

155. Rouse to Professor Elton (6 July 1933). It is to be feared that, attracted by the title, Rouse had bought a copy of Joyce's *Ulysses*.

156. Rouse to Pound (8 February 1935). Beinecke Library, Yale University.

157. Rouse to Pound (21 October 1937). Beinecke Library, Yale University. There is no record of a response to this verdict from Pound.

158. Ibid., letter 7.

159. Pound to Rouse (March 1935). Beinecke Library, Yale University.

160. Pound to Rouse (1936). Beinecke Library, Yale University.

161. Pound to Rouse (24 December 1934).

162. Pound to Rouse, n.d. but ca. 1935. Rouse Papers.

163. Pound to Rouse (27 February 1935). Beinecke Library, Yale University.

164. Rouse, W.H.D., 'A Greek Skipper', *Cambridge Review* (24 May 1906), 414-5. The original is in the Nekuia: *Odyssey* XI.118-35. It is hard to believe that Rouse was unaware of this, but he makes no reference to it in his article.

165. Pound to Rouse (24 December 1934). Rouse Papers.

166. Pound to Rouse (?January 1935). Rouse Papers.

167. Pound to Rouse (18 March 1935). Beinecke Library, Yale University.

168. Pound to Rouse (February 1935). Beinecke Library, Yale University.

169. Pound to Rouse (10 April 1935). Beinecke Library, Yale University.

170. Pound to Rouse (April 1935). Beinecke Library, Yale University.

171. Pound to Rouse (February 1935). Beinecke Library, Yale University.

172. Pound to Rouse (18 March 1935). Beinecke Library, Yale University.

173. Pound to Rouse (June 1937). Beinecke Library, Yale University.

174. Montgomery Butchart to Rouse (23 August 1937). Rouse Papers, box 113[ii], Christ's College, Cambridge.

175. Rouse to Lind (1947). Ibid.

176. Lind to Rouse (13 October 1940). Rouse Papers.

177. Sayers to Rouse (22 December 1948). Rouse Papers.

178. Information from Dr Michael Lockwood, F.W. Lockwood's son and Rouse's godson.

179. These were written in collaboration with Arthur Munday, who, as a pupil of Lockwood, represented the next generation of Rousean epigoni.

180. In particular, the humanities element in Peckett's course attracted support from the chief Classics Inspector, Charles Baty, whose wife was Polish and who was himself keen on linking Classics with the European cultural tradition as a whole.

181. It should be emphasised that Peckett and Lockwood are only two of a larger group of pupils who went on to spread Rouse's message in schools, even though not all were classicists. They include Arthur Eagling, Donald Hughes and John Mitchell. The last-named wrote the standard modern history of the Perse School and was a Fellow of Rouse's old college, Christ's, Cambridge.

182. *The Pelican* (1950), 751-3.

183. Green, P., *Kenneth Grahame 1859-1932* (Murray, 1959), 2.

184. Ibid., pp. 26, 44.

185. Green makes interesting use of the comparison between Grahame and Dodgson in his biography of the former, *passim*.

186. A.W. Verrall, in his chapter in C. Jebb, *Life of Sir R.C. Jebb OM* (Cambridge University Press, 1907).

187. See Butler, M., *Peacock Displayed* (Routledge, 1979), 1- 25.

188. E.R. Dodds, quoted in R. Ellmann, *Oscar Wilde* (H. Hamilton, 1987), 103.

189. Green, P., *Kenneth Grahame*, 121.

190. Ackermann, R.A., 'Some letters of the Cambridge Ritualists', *Greek, Roman and Byzantine Studies* 12 (1971), 113-36.

191. Fowler to Rouse, letters 1905-9, *passim*. Rouse Papers.

192. This is not the place for a discussion of the HMIs' policies. But it should be mentioned that they confronted a genuine difficulty: while the Board consistently supported the inclusion of Latin in secondary curricula, there was a severe shortage of teachers who were qualified in Classics. One of the motives behind resistance to the Direct Method was thus the concern to support courses which were 'teacher-proof': that is, did not depend for their success on a teacher's personal qualities and experience.

193. This is apparent in, for example, the report of the Schools Sub-committee of the Classical Association, 1938 (CA Archives), and in

Failure of the 4-year course, report of classical HMIs' meeting (4-5 April 1945). Public Record Office, Ed 158/52: Classics panel (1933-9, 1944-51).

194. For the remark, and for a general discussion of contemporary changes in classical education, see C.A. Stray, 'Culture or discipline? the redefinition of classical education', in (ed.) M.H. Price, *The Development of the Secondary Curriculum* (Croom Helm, 1986), 10-48.